70001665203 0

ONEWORLD BEGINNER'S GUIDES combine an original, inventive and engaging approach with expert analysis. Innovative and affordable, books in the series are perfect for anyone curious about the way the world works and the big ideas of our time.

History

A Beginner's Guide

David Nash

ONEWORLD

A Oneworld Paperback Original

Published in North America, Great Britain and Australia by
Oneworld Publications, 2016

Copyright © David Nash 2016

The moral right of David Nash to be identified as the Author
of this work has been asserted by him in accordance with the
Copyright, Designs and Patents Act 1988

ISBN 978-1-78074-802-3
eISBN 978-1-78074-803-0

Typeset by Silicon Chips
Printed and bound in Great Britain
by Clays Ltd, St Ives plc

Oneworld Publications
10 Bloomsbury Street

For my sister Barbara Tallis

who introduced hundreds to history and still does

Contents

1

Introduction

History without doubt brightens and enriches our contemporary world. It enables us to see and discover both physical and psychological aspects of ourselves located in another place – the past. Beyond the familiar, that past can also seem enticing, distant, and exotic. Frequently it is this blend of the familiar and the exotic that has been the central reason for making history popular with people at large.

History is a sometimes daunting and overwhelming subject that has many different shapes for many different people. At the grandest scale it can explain the changes that have occurred to vast empires, countries, and continents over centuries or even millennia. At the other end of the scale it can also chart the experience of individual people, sometimes over a few days or even hours. Yet history also deals with cultures on these twin levels of magnitude. It can chart the history of a race or a people over a similar timespan, or trace what has happened to individual cultural beliefs over a few short years. It can tell stories about the concrete artefacts of our past (objects, works of literature, buildings) or follow the evolution and change of the most intangible of emotions. History spreads itself over a vast canvas of our existence to shape and make sense somehow of all that has happened to this planet and its inhabitants. But it is also a search for the truth about the past, something the nineteenth-century

English constitutional historian William Stubbs considered to be one of history's great charms and perhaps its very greatest temptation. As such it is difficult to escape from history's reach and its touch. History, in some way, is a part of every living thing on this planet and its impact is impossible to evade.

However, exploring this dimension is in danger of making history sound as though it is purely something that happens to us without our consent, or even sometimes our knowledge – as though it were some unseen force at work within the universe. Yet it is possible to be actively empowered by history if we choose to understand its processes and to make it coherent as people have done since the very earliest times. History can also be enthralling, engaging, and fun – all that is required to start experiencing it in this manner is curiosity and a willingness to follow our thoughts and explorations to their natural conclusions.

If you, the reader, have this curiosity, you certainly want to know more, but perhaps you are unsure about how to dip your toe into the potentially dark and deep waters of historical studies. This book aims to make this process easy without the risk of the reader ever feeling out of their depth. This, then, is a gentle introduction, but one that nonetheless has a robust and serious intention: to enable the individual to embark on their own discovery of the past. This is because, for many of us, a passing interest in history is simply not enough. We crave a greater depth of knowledge and the opportunity to understand what makes history tick, and to ensure the experience of history is as valuable and enriching as possible for all of us.

Craving a depth of knowledge and insight into what makes history tick explains why historical narratives are so regularly fictionalized in novels, on the cinema screen and on television. These ambitiously hope to make history cross over from knowledge and investigation into the world of entertainment. Although it is interesting to plunge into what such narratives can tell us, really this is the creation of a 'history lite' species that only gives us a mere flavour of the past. This past is a portrayal and spectacle. However, building real knowledge and explanations is a different enterprise and this is what we actively call history.

The popular writing of history regularly stimulates the imagination and each year new magazines are launched which cover ever-widening aspects of the subject. The last twenty years has also seen a dramatic upsurge in television coverage and investigation of history and the reasons for this are not really very hard to find. The past can be an intensely visual subject and many documentaries have concentrated on the physical and visual residue of the past. Documentaries on the eighteenth-century English country house, for example, have been able to show lavish interiors and furnishings, and to speculate about the manner of life that went on in these surroundings. The preoccupation with this has also been stimulated by a wave of costume dramas that focus on the past as a place where universal human actions are played out. Other factual television programmes try and bring the past to life by juxtaposing individual stories with a look at locations as they appear today. This particular tendency has been a feature of television coverage of the centenary of the outbreak of the First World War. Television has also developed the genre of the personal journey, in which an individual investigates the past through their own ancestors and their own life stories. A once-again-fashionable way in which people encounter popular history has been through the historical 'scoop' story, or the attempt to find a solution or resolution to a long-running historical puzzle or mystery. The most recent examples of this include the apparent discovery of Richard III's body buried beneath a Leicester council car park and the supposed unmasking of Jack the Ripper through the use of forensic evidence.

Whilst these often provide fascinating entertainment, and glimpses of real insight, some people watching them often wish for a still greater level of understanding of the history these phenomena represent. Does this display and outline of history ask enough deep and penetrating questions? Are these displays taking into account different approaches and aspects of the history they try to explain and portray? Lastly, whether it is a presentation of the eighteenth-century country house or the solution to a historical whodunnit, many ask whether these are telling the whole story, or indeed the truth, and how far we should allow these representations to claim that they are definitive. The eighteenth-century country house and the lavish wealth needed to fill, furnish and support it was arguably accumulated through applying increasingly tough farming and market practices. These marginalized and removed rights from poor members of the population living on subsistence land and lifestyles based on grazing and foraging. Likewise the rapid haste with which the solution to the Jack the Ripper case was trumpeted by the *Daily Mail* in September 2014 reflected a journalistic urge to provide a solution to the murders, rather than think deeply about the supposed facts being presented. Not only was DNA taken from a discredited source, but it was also mistakenly traced to the descendants of the wrong man with the same name! Besides, actually finding the identity of Jack the Ripper would not answer some of the wider and more important questions about Victorian England thrown up by the case. Why did these murders attract publicity when others did not? Indeed, the continuing fascination with this particular case, stretching well over a century, actually has its own history. Once we begin to think more deeply for ourselves about the questions generated by history, we become less satisfied with its presentation in magazines and on television and the easy answers they offer. In short, we wish to know more, to be capable of analysing and thinking more deeply about the material and answers history gives us. Ultimately it is not surprising that we ask more sophisticated questions because, unless we do, history portrayed as spectacle becomes merely superficial mood music.

So what is this 'history' we are all so interested in? Many generations of scholars have wrestled with precisely this question, not always profitably. This would suggest it is an extremely difficult and problematic question to answer with the clarity and brevity required by this book. Thus rather than tie us up unnecessarily with preliminary material about the subject's origins or dry discussions about its definition, this book has attempted to tackle these questions with a self-conscious 'learning by doing' approach. What this really means is that most of the central aspects of history are tackled through the use of illustrative examples and stories. By following and understanding the stories outlined below, the reader will engage with, think through, and pick up many of the essential technical elements that every good historian needs to make sense of the past.

This book has opted to divide its approaches to history, and the examples used to illustrate this, into chapters about people and events, and those about everyday objects. This is a method of both exploring different approaches to history and illustrating aspects of the great variety of history. Both of these serve to demonstrate that everything has a history, and by tuning your mind to the types of sources and explanations associated with almost anything, you can think about or trace its history.

This division also has another purpose, since the study of people in the past and the events that have involved them is clearly fundamentally important to understanding the growth and development of human society. The thoughts and actions of people have left a vitally important imprint on the historical record of all societies throughout time. Most of this imprint seems deliberately calculated – that the conscious thoughts and actions of individuals play themselves out in the records they have left behind and the events of which they tell. However, considering the history of objects opens up the opportunity to consider phenomena where the conscious imprint of humankind is less obvious. Whilst an object may be created by an individual, its subsequent use and purpose may not exhibit the intention of its creator, even within the lifetime of that creator. Likewise our own thoughts about objects themselves change from age to age, and it is often the case that the history of objects can tell us as much about a period of history as the conscious created histories and the intentions of that age deliberately expressed in the historical record.

The examples in this book stand on their own merit as good stories (always a fundamentally valuable and important start). However, they should also prove sufficiently interesting and intriguing that the reader scarcely notices she or he is learning these approaches and mechanisms as we proceed. By the end of the book the reader will have acquired a basic toolkit of techniques, ideas, and approaches that will enable them to embark on a deeper and more sophisticated study, and appreciation, of history. These realized concrete examples will also function as a reference point of explanation when thinking about further pieces and episodes of history beyond the coverage of this book.

Nonetheless, we cannot escape definitions entirely and should still say that the most useful definition of history is that it is an attempt to understand and make coherent sense of the past. This statement might seem obvious but it is difficult to overestimate its importance. It is sometimes jokingly suggested that history is 'just one damned thing after another' but within this exasperation is a simple humorous message that is nevertheless still important. If we simply view events and the past as some sort of hurricane, which blows past us, we are failing to understand our world and what has made it the way it is. So the investigation, study, and communication of history take upon themselves the task of explaining the past. Through these activities we catalogue the past and create a narrative about what happened. Sometimes this is a chronology and sometimes it is the examination of the past as an artefact, such as the study of mentalities or of material culture, which adopt different starting points.

A chronology is essentially a timeline of the sequence in which events happened or occurred. However, once this sequence has been established it is a starting point for finding an explanation of why things happen. Raising questions about this and answering these is what gives us our explanation of what happened in the past and why. So we must be careful that the central questions about the past we create are important and do their job. It is the nature of these questions that helps us realize the difference between history and the past. The past is a list of events and it can often be extremely important to know this sequence, because this is often the central building block upon which history is built. History itself is frequently the explanation for these events, and sometimes the sequence in which they occur. However, we should also remember that some historical investigations (of customs, of practices, and of past institutions) involve the recreation of a system, or a state of mind, where chronology may not actually seem important at all.

Creating such a chronological sequence relies on the concept of causality – namely what factor caused a particular event in history to happen. For example, tracing causes can offer an explanation unknown to contemporaries in the past. In the early nineteenth century Western Europe was visited by a wave of Asiatic cholera which killed many thousands in cities from Russia through to Great Britain. Cholera had never spread this far west before and historians went in search of explanations for this phenomenon. They were able to trace the origin (or cause) of this to recent changes in irrigation practices, which had been encouraged by the British Raj in northern India. These had left abundant quantities of stagnant water in which the disease could flourish – the connectedness of imperial trade routes did the rest!

Before the investigation of causes, our initial and obvious questions concern issues about when things happened and who was involved in them. Whilst it may seem important to know the date when a battle occurred, when a piece of important social legislation was passed, or when an individual died, this is only because we need to establish when this event occurred in relation to other events. Similarly we will most often find that the lives and actions of individuals are only important in relation to how they interacted with other people. As we gain more and greater understanding, we will find that our central questions move away from the issues around dates and individuals to look at wider questions that explain ideas, systems, and processes. We may well know the precise dates of the First World War but it becomes of greater significance to ask what caused it. Whilst instinct might suggest that life is made easier by searching for one single cause to which we can attribute the event, we rapidly learn from historians that the matter is considerably more complex. Political historians might talk about Great Power rivalries, whilst military historians would perhaps cite a hopelessly out-of-control arms race. Meanwhile economic historians might suggest the war was perhaps an episode in a longer struggle for economic dominance in the West. Thus, with nearly all history, we can find ourselves trying to evaluate the relative merits of multiple possible causes.

We should also be aware that constructing a chronology is not a neutral exercise and can equally be influenced by the precise subject the historian wishes to investigate. This can also be a place where bias, methodological preference, ideology, and the particular approach adopted by a historian influences the chronology they might construct. Historians investigating the reasons for the rise of Nazi Germany might want to focus on Hitler's rise to power. However, others might go further back and seek to include the failure of the League of Nations to deal adequately with Germany as instrumental in this development. Others might go further back to the problems associated with the Treaty of Versailles and its treatment of Germany after its defeat in the First World War. However, some, like the social historian Richard Grunberger, look further back into the nineteenth century and see the rise of Nazism as caused by the failure of Germany to develop a middle class in the manner of other Western countries.

History is sometimes said to have particular wider aims. Although these were slightly more fashionable in the earlier part of the twentieth century, it is worth noting these so that readers can decide their value for themselves. One possible aim is to consider how much an investigation of history provides us all with valuable knowledge of human experience. Thus history serves as the accumulated human experience of past ages – a vast cultural resource from which we can all draw insights and lessons. Some historians also argue that this accumulation of experience needs to be labelled, categorized, and identified to allow some of its uniqueness to speak to the present. This has given birth to the history of minority groups which includes everything from the history of individual nations, through the history of classes, races, and ethnicities, the indigenous and the alien, to the different genders and sexual orientations.

For most of the last millennium another dominant approach which emphasized the value of history and historical study was to equate it with the idea of progress. This is sometimes referred to as Whig history, which argued that we live in the 'best of all possible worlds'. The eighteenth-century German historian Leopold von Ranke suggested that this 'best of all possible worlds' idea was so often repeated that the writing of history was likely to continue reflecting it far beyond his own time. This idea, which is of some antiquity, argued that life for mankind was getting better with each successive age. It looked backwards frequently to see the past as a series of older, often archaic practices and lifestyles which modern human ingenuity had either outgrown or replaced with better, improved practices or lifestyles. Thus the evolution of parliamentary democracy in most Western states could be shown, by this approach to history, to be an apparent improvement upon early modern despotism or the social and economic problems of feudal society. Such apparently modern democratic societies could also readily point to their track record of prosperity alongside a quite impressive history of social and political peace.

The medieval world had its own idea of progress since it considered history as capable of demonstrating the Christian God's plan for mankind, unfolding before the eyes of successive generations. From the seventeenth century onwards the Enlightenment gave birth to a different idea of progress, in which human discoveries and ingenuity were capable of changing the world for the better, as von Ranke also suggested. Discoveries, such as Newton's assertion that the universe was in balance and self-regulating, argued that divine intervention was no longer a central part of existence. Progress was also demonstrated through technological advancement (such as the invention and application of steam power) and increasing the productivity of agriculture through innovations in arable farming, and the advent of selective breeding of livestock. There was also a greater level of sophistication and achievement in the world of the arts and an apparently endless capability to improve the material well-being of the whole species through the growth of commerce.

Progress, as we have discovered, is the ability to measure the achievements of a historical period against those of the past. Those who subscribe to the idea of progress hold the unwavering belief that the present conditions of life for men and women are an improvement upon previous periods of history. Certainly, if we look at things like life expectancy, everyday health, and general levels of prosperity, we might justifiably conclude things are better for us than they were in the average nineteenth-century city. In many respects this comparison is also confirmed by our historical investigations of the nineteenth-century city. This will invariably turn up a story of poor sanitation, overcrowding, and aspects of the infrastructure that were either undeveloped or dysfunctional. Against such a background, the achievements of the average twenty-first-century city would admirably fit the definition of progress. However, it is worth thinking about how far such definitions are Westernized and biased towards the northern hemisphere. Whilst material prosperity and the extension of this has been the West's story, we might look at other areas of the world that have slid from prosperity in the past into relative poverty in the present. Indeed some individuals might argue the true measure of the West's progress is to be found in its ability to address the problems of Third World poverty – this would be a real measure of both civilization and progress simultaneously.

Many who believed in the idea of progress almost invariably saw it as an unchanging, all-embracing phenomenon. For these people a belief in progress meant that improvement was happening in every area of society and life. Von Ranke also noted this folly, writing that it was a fundamental mistake to believe 'that all the branches of human experience and knowledge have developed throughout the centuries at the same rate'. The study of history very frequently alters this picture and shows progress is, at the very least, uneven, and at its worst messy and contradictory. Moreover the assumption that all developments are automatically an improvement can sometimes be mistaken. If we were to look at medical developments that have improved our ability to treat once dangerous life-threatening illnesses, even these sometimes do not easily fit into a definition of progress because subsequent events can outflank this idea. When antibiotics became widely available they were rightly hailed as a real step forward in treating infection. However, we have now discovered that within a few generations their over-prescription and overuse has rendered them markedly less effective. As a result, some of the infectious illnesses they used to treat are making something of a resurgence. History would scarcely have argued that their invention was a mistake. Nonetheless what history does tell us is that the actual story of their invention, introduction, and widespread use is far more complex than simply noting their intended purpose as a type of progress. Likewise, whilst housing conditions improved markedly for most people in the West, rising populations make overcrowding an even harsher reality in other parts of the planet.

Here again the story of housing improvement is not as simple as the idea of progress might lead us to believe.

Leopold von Ranke also noted how the idea of progress could encourage people to take an artificial and unjustifiably poor view of the past. He argued that the obsession with progress would invariably see past generations as the embarrassingly poor relations of those living in the present. The idea that 'every generation is more perfect than the preceding one' von Ranke deemed 'a divine injustice' that would also render the past as having 'no significance in and for itself. It would become meaningful only insofar as it became the steppingstone [sic] to the next generation'. Concentrating on this uneven and messy nature of progress sometimes leads historians to see other patterns and destinations by no means linked with the idea of progress – these are often referred to as teleologies. Some wonder what the shape of these connections is likely to resemble. Many see teleologies as straight lines, although von Ranke considered them 'more like a stream, whose course winds about in its own way'. One such pattern, which has been a preoccupation of Western societies for some years now, has been the supposed implications of global warming and climate change. Those who believe climate change to be a reality argue that greenhouse gases have been increasingly produced by human activity since the Industrial Revolution. This has intensified during the course of the twentieth century and, based on their knowledge of past data, they feel confident enough to predict a rise in global temperature and an alteration in weather patterns. These changes will themselves also serve to alter existing patterns of life on the planet.

However, following from the previous example, not all teleologies result in eventual pessimism. In 1968 a group of scientists, industrialists, and economists formed an organization called the Club of Rome. This group stated its aim was to think about issues and problems facing the planet in the medium-term future. In 1972 this group published a bombshell report entitled *The Limits to Growth*. This was a wide-ranging and deeply pessimistic view that human activity was going to run out of raw materials and resources, meaning that civilization would effectively fall off a cliff. One important part of this analysis was its investigation of previous patterns of human consumption, and from this they proposed theories about the rate at which natural resources had been used up by human activity in the past. The Club went on to argue that such reckless consumption was unsustainable beyond the following decade. This was teleology, not unlike environmentalism, which predicted the collapse of human society and eventual extinction. Very quickly this teleology was criticized by a conflicting one. This argued that the scarcity of resources would inspire human ingenuity to find and exploit hitherto untapped ones, to exploit better the ones that it already had available, or indeed to do without them altogether. As it has turned out, the rapid extinction predicted by the Club of Rome has been countered by such adaptability and innovation. However, the Club of Rome might plausibly offer the counterargument that the situation has merely been slowed down or temporarily postponed. Certainly one implication of this example is that the production of teleologies can help with finding patterns in the past and thinking about how the future might actually follow these, even if it becomes almost impossible actually to predict this with certainty.

History: the ultimate social science or an art form?

Human society has constantly grappled with the idea of history fulfilling two functions. Firstly, it is frequently seen as, above all other things, a narrative – in other words, a story outlining events, generally ordered to suggest some particular message or to make some particular factor important. However, another school of thought suggests that history is one of the social sciences and so is able to provide us with an empirical and quantified fact-based explanation of the truth, even if this truth could sometimes be uncomfortable. Von Ranke suggested this 'strict presentation of the facts, contingent and unattractive though they may be, is the highest law'. In some respects these views, that history was both fact and narrative, were for many years compatible. Those who embraced one of these two particular schools of thought brought their preferences to bear upon the type of history they chose to study and chose to write about. This also tended to influence the branch of history individuals found themselves researching.

There are many spheres of human activity in modern civilization so it is not surprising to find there are many branches of history, many consciously constructed to reflect precisely this diversity of human activity. Thus economic history looks at the history of human economic activity. This can look at everything from an individual's economic situation to that of an individual business, or industry, right up to the economic state of a whole nation. Much of economic history, but crucially not all of it, involves elements of counting and comparison. Thus economic history very frequently uses methods of determining levels of price, income, consumption, and prosperity. However, economic history also looks at the development of financial and trading systems as well as systems of consumption. Very clearly a part of this is also assessing what individuals and past societies thought of all of these systems and chose to operate within them.

Social history is the history of societies in the past and the activities within society's social spaces in which individuals were involved. This can include everything from shared experiences of the workplace, of leisure and consumption patterns, right through to the shared experiences of life (birth, marriage, divorce, and death). Thus social historians are much more likely to use sources such as diaries, newspapers, and personal testimony. However, it should be noted that social history itself scarcely rules out the potential use of quantitative methods to count the social and cultural meaning of consumption or such things as leisure patterns and other aspects of the life cycle. Because social history obviously deals with the social, it is also more likely to use some of the tools associated with the social sciences. Thus elements of sociology (or anthropology) that classify groups of people are of considerable use to the social historian characterizing the shared attitudes and behaviours of groups in past society. Likewise historians of crime may well find themselves interested in the ideas of criminologists and psychologists about criminal behaviour and its patterns. Political history, whilst it often investigates the actions of politicians and their effects, will also potentially use methodology from political science and international relations.

However, there are also branches of history that draw on older intellectual traditions and the formulation of how we discover and analyse the world. One such branch of history, which is also of considerable antiquity, is the history of how ideas, thoughts, and the process of thinking have altered. This is sometimes called intellectual history or the history of ideas. This looks at the work of thinkers whose ideas influenced or changed the society of their times or sometimes just after. Equally part of this history is the examination of how some ideas come to be rendered obsolete by events or changes in thinking. In the post-war world, for example, South Africa implemented the ideology of apartheid. This rigid and enforced racial segregation was supposedly for the benefit of all races. It was not simply a political ideology, since it also had intellectuals who were prepared to borrow ideas about the supremacy of some races over others from Nazi Germany. This set of ideas had its roots in the study of eugenics – the quest to improve the quality of the human population. This idea of eugenics had originated in the nineteenth century and it passed through many hands after this point. It was seriously considered by everyone from British government ministers, to socialists, nationalists, Nazis and other fascists, and democracies throughout the twentieth century. It is worth remembering that such ideas could inspire utopian dreams of breeding out poverty and removing disability and debilitating illness, as well as the nightmares of selective breeding, racial purity, and ideas of a master race. Very often such ideas would fall out of favour and be superseded by others, only to reappear somewhere else in another guise. In the case of South Africa, apartheid became discredited as a political system and was overtaken and smothered by newer, conflicting ideas of racial equality, self-determination, and multiculturalism.

Likewise intellectual history often looks at how even apparently simple ideas are both unconsciously and consciously made to inspire subsequent generations. One example of this is provided by the ideas associated with the eighteenth-century economist Adam Smith. He noted in a widely read and much reprinted book, *The Wealth of Nations*, that subdividing labour in factories could greatly increase output and trade. The importance of this idea fuelled the development of factories and production lines right through to Henry Ford in the twentieth century and beyond. The very latest manifestation of this simple idea appears on the current English £20 note. This has a profile portrait of Adam Smith, with his dates underneath (1723–90), beside a picture of the first production line that Smith had encountered which embodied the division of labour he so greatly admired. Beneath this is an explanation of the picture as a depiction of 'the division of labour in pin manufacturing: (and the great increase in the quantity of work that results)'. This remains an obviously simple idea easily communicated to subsequent generations. Putting it on the £20 note seems somehow deliberate since it conveys the idea of economic success enabled by simple but effective innovation – arguably the recipe for success and economic growth within any developing economy.

Historians adopt different views about the type of evidence they should use to investigate historical phenomena. Those who want to investigate the level of religious belief within a past society might choose to use a range of different evidence dependent upon their attitude to this evidence. Some historians have used lists of those taking communion as a measure of religious devotion at a particular time in the past. Ironically many pious members of society would simply not be included on this list. They would be missing because their deeply ingrained conception of their own sin would prevent them from taking communion, thus excluding themselves from a source eventually used to measure religious devotion. But the problems do not stop there. Of those who did take communion, many may well have embraced the sacrament for a variety of reasons which might have included maintaining the visible display of belief, to maintain social status, or simply out of sheer habit. Although historians using these records cannot know these reasons, they do cast doubt on the apparent certainty of using communion numbers as a straightforward test of the level of religious belief within a past society. Others would prefer to look at the levels of popular belief in things like superstitious habits, customs, and rites of passage. Very frequently these are offshoots of connections with official religious belief. However, the fact that these are more readily practised in the home and elsewhere suggests a more genuine attachment to religious belief than counting those who take communion might suggest. By no means are any of these historians more obviously 'correct' in their assumptions than their colleagues who do something different. However, what they have chosen is their best guess at what will give the most meaningful and accurate picture. In making this choice they are showing an awareness of the problems associated with the approaches they have actively chosen not to use. Sometimes this choice can be influenced by bias about the reliability of methods or by an ideological preference for one technique over another. A social historian interested in ideas associated with 'history from below' will more readily embrace the idea of exploring superstition and custom, since this evidence appears more readily generated from below.

'HISTORY FROM BELOW'

History from below was championed by left-wing historians who, encouraged by the expansion of university education in the 1960s, tried to rescue the history of common people who they felt had been written out of previous histories, which concentrated on great men and high politics. This challenge to conventional history would later be supported by new histories of ethnic minorities and women which likewise argued they had been marginalized in the historical record.

Similarly, communion records seem less attractive to this type of historian because they are constructed by an official organization (in this case the Church) and thus generated 'from above' (no pun intended). This, however, might be precisely the reason why a historian of the Church as an institution may actively want to use such records.

However, some approaches to specific forms of history are more closely tied to ideology than the methodology of other social sciences. Gender history, for example, originally sprang from feminist history which argued that the writing of history had been significantly dominated by men to the active exclusion of women, their interests, and their importance. Another ideological approach that has had a significant impact on the practice and writing of history has been Marxism. This essentially absorbed Karl Marx's idea that at the bottom of human motivation lay economic motives. He argued that these inspired, and were the very fabric of, all human activity. He also argued that significant economic changes were fundamental to the evolving nature of human society. His ideas were also related to the idea of teleology since he argued that human development would go through a number of stages. The first of these stages would be characterized by feudal societies where agrarian activity dominated and there was almost no such thing as economic growth. This, so Marx argued, would be followed by the development of commercial and industrial capitalism which introduced mass production and the mass employment of individuals who could only make a living by selling their labour. Marx referred to this group of people as the proletariat who he believed would be, because of their lowly economic status, alienated from the society in which they lived and toiled. Ultimately this alienation would motivate them to rise up and overthrow capitalism to achieve a communist society in which all property was owned communally.

Here we can see a marriage of ideological, thematic, and methodological approaches in how a certain type of historian might choose to study a certain type of history. Marxist historians can write about more or less anything, but they are especially drawn to the history around dramatic changes such as revolutions. This is largely because, in their model of change, both the idea and reality of conflict played a very important role. A new idea, or form of society (what Marx called the thesis), would conflict with an older form (the anti-thesis), and this clash would produce a third form (the synthesis). Thus with an interest in types of conflict Marxist historians might well draw on political history to investigate new political ideologies that would mark a transition from one stage of society to the next. Likewise, they are interested in the process by which social classes are created, since this is also likely to indicate types of change coming to a society. The Marxist historian Christopher Hill put these two types of analysis together to produce a Marxist interpretation of what many historians refer to as the English Civil War (more recently named the War of the Three Kingdoms). Hill saw this significant upheaval in English, Scottish, and Irish history as having its root causes in the developing social structure of the period. He suggested that a new class (roughly corresponding to a type of middle class) was trying to emerge within British society. They wanted to overthrow the tyranny of the landed interests in favour of promoting commerce, trade, and industry for their own benefit. Such a development would have been a step on the road towards the eventual realization of a communist society. For a historian like Hill, the English Civil War happened because this new class had its opportunities to take power and change society actively blocked by the survival of older interests. An important part of this struggle for Hill (and for all Marxist historians) was that this new class realized its interest and identity in what this analysis regularly referred to as class consciousness. Marxist historians were also responsible for a similar reading of the French Revolution at the end of the eighteenth century, which they saw as creating what would later be described as bourgeois society in nineteenth-century France.

Marxist history is less fashionable now than it once was, and certainly many who take issue with it have voiced their concerns about accepting that economics is at the bottom of everything. Although there were individual rejections of the Marxist interpretations of the English Civil War and French Revolution, there were also other challenges to Marxism. One of these, which actively rejected Marxism, saw language at the bottom of human activity rather than economics. This challenge to Marxism was called structuralism, appearing later in a variant form called post-structuralism. Whilst the Marxist historian could identify social classes because they were created by economic conditions, a post-structuralist argued that this reality did not exist outside the historical source or text. In other words this latter viewpoint saw the text itself as creating the reality so that the idea of class, which had one meaning for a Marxist, could have multiple meanings for a structuralist. This is because the idea of class seems to appear in different documents and appears to relate to different contexts and circumstances. Thus the study of language lay at the bottom of meaning in history for structuralists and post-structuralists; different individuals operated with different meanings even though they may well have used the same words. Because of this difficulty post-structuralists came to reject the idea of a definitive meaning that enables us to construct a truth about the past. This has been a significant challenge to much conventional history which, after all, seeks to provide an explanation that we believe to be the truth. This, we should now remember, is based on a mixture of facts, sources, interpretation, and bias woven into an interpretation that seeks to tell the truth. Whilst post-structuralists argue this idea of truth is an illusion, they do leave themselves open to the accusation that they do not themselves offer a more credible, more likely, and apparently more 'truthful' alternative. In this sense their analysis relies as much on likelihood as any other form of analysis that strives to seek the truth about history and historical events.

History as a creative activity

Several classical and medieval historians demonstrated that history and its writing could be an art form, with everything around its imagining and its creation that this implies. Looking at a Roman historian such as Tacitus (56–117 CE), who gave ancient Rome its first description of Britain, we can see that both events and the story he told were created and ordered to achieve a number of tasks. Tacitus was anxious to portray the near contemporary Roman imperial governor of Britain, Agricola (40–93 CE), as a talented and able individual – scarcely surprising since the latter was his father-in-law! In order to make Agricola and his actions appear heroic, Tacitus uses some of the tools any story writer would instinctively reach for. He gives us a physical description of Agricola so that we might more readily picture and believe in the character so described.

As to his personal appearance – in case the interest of posterity should extend to such a matter – he was good-looking rather than striking. His features did not indicate a passionate nature: the prevailing impression was one of charm. There was no difficulty about recognizing him as a good man, and one could willingly believe him to be a great man. Though he was taken from us in the prime of his vigorous manhood, yet, so far as glory is concerned, the longest span of years could not have made his life more complete.

Yet how does Tacitus suggest to us that Agricola's life could not have been more complete? He does this by showing his father-in-law's effective conquest of Britain and his talent in subjugating the tribes he found there. In the story this task is achieved by suggesting how ineffective and lacklustre previous attempts to conquer Britain had actually been. The Romans' first contact with the islands of Britain had occurred in 55 BCE when Julius Caesar explored the southern portion of it. Tacitus suggests Caesar's expedition had 'merely drawn attention to it' whilst a subsequent emperor, Gaius, made elaborate plans to annex the country, although these were shelved as other priorities surfaced elsewhere in the Empire. Britain was eventually subdued by the Emperor Claudius, but there were also frequent rebellions culminating in the East Anglian Queen Boudicca's destruction of several Roman outposts. Tacitus here suggests the powerful nature of this rebellion both to strike fear in his Roman readership and to prepare the way for the later triumph of Agricola in the story.

Egged on by such mutual encouragements, the whole island rose under the leadership of Boudicca, a lady of royal descent – for Britons make no distinction of sex in their appointment of commanders. They hunted down the Roman troops in their scattered posts, stormed the forts, and assaulted the colony itself, which they saw as the citadel of this servitude; and there was no form of savage cruelty that the angry victors refrained from.

The story then follows the description of seven years in which the bravery, intelligence, good sense, and professionalism of Agricola enabled the Roman armies to defeat all opposition in England as well as parts of Wales and Scotland. The story ends with Agricola's death and suggests he was not necessarily mourned by his emperor Domitian, who had grown jealous of his abilities and success. It may have been that Tacitus wrote this history to safeguard his father-in-law's memory or perhaps even to enhance it. Thus we have a story here that uses description, narrative, and analysis to present a coherent and complete history. Its writer obviously selected facts, employed techniques of storytelling, and used them to achieve specific purposes.

This is an example of history as a practised art, but it is also a history deliberately constructed for a purpose. As such it asks us questions about how far we believe the story being told and it makes us wary that what we are reading might be biased. Certainly more recent times have also seen history used consciously as a tool of propaganda. Soviet Russia in the early part of the twentieth century used history to marginalize groups it considered bourgeois and dangerous to the security of the revolution, such as smallholding farmers (the Kulaks). It would also do this with individuals who were inconvenient to subsequent Soviet regimes. Leon Trotsky was famously removed from a number of iconic photographs in an attempt to present an alternative history of the Soviet state that had been created without his contribution to the revolutionary period.

At the opposite end of the spectrum, some historians would prefer to focus on facts and what they see as the power of these to tell history as truth. This becomes obvious when we look at some aspects of social science-informed history, such as social history or economic history. If we revisit our investigation of the history of religion in the West, historians are concerned to analyse what religious observance and belief are like today in relation to how they have been in the past. Many historians looked at the declining place of Christianity within Western culture as a distinct and important indication that it was no longer as important as it once had been. They looked at the development of modern society as a series of areas and institutions from which Christianity could be said to have retreated. The Church was no longer responsible for aspects of health and welfare of the population at large in the way it had been during the medieval period. Similarly churches were no longer responsible for the provision of education, which had increasingly become the responsibility of the state. Such historians called this process secularization, and they believed they could chart its progress through different Western societies over a three-hundred-year period.

From the early nineteenth century, figures measuring church attendance were available, and even from the middle of the century a number of religious censuses actively told historians the condition of Christianity within the towns, cities, and rural parishes of Western Europe. Using these data alongside data for the twentieth century, it seemed possible to create a convincing picture of overall decline albeit with occasional revivals. Within this framework some historians argued about the precise timing of such a decline, whilst others would point to differences in the rate of decline within specific countries, regions, or religious groups. Some even created a narrative in which decline was a remarkably recent phenomenon that would result in Christianity's catastrophic collapse. It seemed possible to do this with the application of numerical data on church attendance and the stated belief of those who were interviewed by researchers, or other written data from the historical past.

However, by using other methods of research, the picture does not look nearly so obvious or clear cut. Church attendance quite obviously does not equate with religious belief, especially since the dawn of the twentieth century. Indeed this century could be said to have ushered in an age when the different ways of being religious multiplied as people came to construct their own religious beliefs and emotions quite independent of traditional religious institutions. In the modern world they form congregations almost invisible to the traditional researcher used to looking for steeple, tower, or even modest hall as the traditional home of organized religion. Attention has also focused on the range of beliefs and superstitions that people have always carried with them as part of their emotional makeup. Some attention has also been directed at how stressful situations, such as wartime, can persuade people to believe more readily in the concept of divine intervention. This was something which should have been consigned to the dustbin of history, if traditional secularization advocates were to be believed. Thus, in terms of the secularization debate, numbers tell us one story and yet examination of more qualitative evidence tells us something profoundly different.

These two different versions and intentions behind history are useful to us not simply because they show two ways that history might be thought about and written, but also because they are ways of investigating one of the arguments that regularly reappears in discussions about the value and purpose of history. In its most modern guise this has been a debate about just how far history can claim to tell the truth about its subject matter. Empirical historians, reliant on facts they consider to be safe and irrefutable, find themselves confronted by those who doubt just how 'true' facts can really be. The first of these types of historian inherits much of the methodology and preoccupations of earlier social science historians, who believed that theories about history were based on facts. The historian more sceptical about the truth of facts is generally influenced by developments in literary studies which have produced so-called postmodern viewpoints. As we will discover, these are a close relative of the structuralist and post-structuralist debates we met a little earlier in this chapter. Like these earlier debates, postmodern ideas are utterly uncertain about the apparent truth of any statement about history and the claims of historians to be using facts that tell a definitive version of the truth. Postmodernism also rejects many of the central stories of so-called modern Western civilization, arguing that they have been discredited. According to these theories, Marxism and Christianity (and for our purposes the scientific quest for truth) are all now questionable and are simply not the truths and explanations that they claimed to be, particularly since, as the argument has it, so many of these 'big theories' were promoted by professional interest groups who wished to retain knowledge solely for themselves. Such theories suggest that the task of history now is simply to catalogue, list, and tell the different stories and narratives that make up history. For these people history is far less likely to explain things and instead comprises a collection, if you like a museum, of the past in all its richness.

Perhaps the best way of seeing how these positions collide and how we can illuminate the preoccupations of both is demonstrated through my attempt to explain this to one of my university classes. On Friday 5 December 2008, I held a class in a certain room at my university at 3.00 PM, on a particularly dull and cold afternoon. Before we started to learn about the postmodern approach to history I asked everybody in the class to write down on a piece of paper why they felt they were actually at that class on that particular Friday afternoon – we were to make use of the answers a little later in the class. I then asked them what would happen if a historian in a year's, or indeed in ten years' time, wanted to investigate this particular class; what evidence would remain that the class ever actually took place? Someone suggested that this historian could actually ask each and every one of the students present about having attended this particular class. I then introduced them to the idea that it was possible that the 'answers' given to this historian could be fabricated lies. Another student suggested that this historian could ask me, the teacher, about this particular class and what had happened within it. Again I had to suggest that I too could be lying about the events of that particular Friday, and that mine would be a biased account because I was an authority figure placed in charge of the story told about this class. Yet another student suggested that this class existed in the course handbook, in the history department's syllabus, and as a slot on the student's own individual computer-generated timetable. From here I had to point out that all of these were documents that suggested only the *intention* to hold the class and the *desire* that it should take place – they did not prove that the class ever actually took place.

What this particular exchange suggested was the precise impact of the postmodernist agenda of questioning 'facts' to undermine them. It graphically suggested and demonstrated that, however secure one felt about the supposed 'truth' of so-called 'facts', their reality was far more open to question than we might otherwise think, even if we were centrally involved in them ourselves! But we were also able to take this example a little further to demonstrate how postmodernists wish to move beyond the illusion of so-called facts. My accounts of the class, its existence in the course guide, as well as the syllabus, and its appearance on the electronic timetable, were all documents created by institutions and figures of authority. Some would describe these as interested, and arguably biased, about the history they would seek to write (just as Tacitus was). It could be suggested that even if these accounts told some element of the truth they were partisan and would not be terribly helpful in writing the history of that particular class on that particular Friday afternoon.

The alternative (arguably postmodern) way to write the history would be to construct and list all the potential narratives produced by, and for, the occasion of that class on Friday 5 December 2008. This is where the preparatory work of the students (their individual list of motives for their attendance at the class) would come in. The alternative view of this class and the history of it lies in the slips of paper the students wrote at the start of the class. I had asked them why they had attended that particular class on that particular day and I was rewarded with a range of answers. Some opted for the obvious instrumental and mechanical explanation – 'it was listed in the course guide and I believed it was important to attend the class'. Others focused more directly on the assessed work they were due to do in pursuit of their grades with statements such as 'I came because I thought I would learn important stuff about the last assignment I have to do'. Some took a slightly broader view with phrases such as 'I want to do well and get a good degree'. Some even took this further with almost a life-plan contained in their response 'I want to do well, get a good university degree, pursue a good career and earn a good wage'. One individual even added the parting phrase 'and be happy!' to their version of this particular motive.

A focus on these narratives by a historian would from here involve them in investigating these slips of paper as 'discourses'. Each of these told a story, but it would be the historian's job to investigate how that story had a wider and deeper historical significance. In seeking to collect 'discourses' this historian would have access to other similar 'discourses' with which to compare them. From here such a historian would be able to tell whether such 'discourses' uttered by my class were typical or something distinct from the norm. Such a historian would also want to know more about the perspective from which each of these 'discourses' had come. Were some things more readily said by the male students than by the female students? Were there also differences between students from different social and educational backgrounds? What of different perspectives influenced by ethnicity or age that were given voice as a result of this classroom task? None of these would contain the series of demonstrable 'truths' that hard-line empirical historians would wish for, and it remains questionable just how 'real' the conclusions from this would be. However, abandoning what this approach argues is the illusion offered by a 'truth'-based explanation rejuvenates the search for deeper historical answers.

The structure of this book

This book moves forward after this chapter to enable us to begin the exploration of how we put history together. This is achieved by two chapters that follow in a logical order. The first of these starts with the idea of historical sources and how all history is ultimately dependent on these. It looks at the range of sources that can be used to investigate a particular universal phenomenon – in this case the idea of love. From this it also explores the power of sources by investigating two counterfeit sources intended to change the historical record. This enables us to realize how a new source might have changed the history we know about two incidents. This potential to change history is showcased here by the fact that these two sources never actually had this impact, but only might have done if they had been real. This fictitious changed history can be much more readily compared to the real history which remains unaltered. We also learn that recognizing historical facts is itself a crucial part of the process of being able to write history. To help us on our way we are introduced to a method of testing the viability of such sources through ideas of credibility, likelihood, and verifiability.

The following chapter investigates issues of causality and explanation through an examination of the numerous theories associated with the assassination of John F. Kennedy in Dallas in November 1963. We then investigate how causes and causality can be thought through by placing them in a hierarchy of plausibility. Investigation of the plausible, for the moment, stays with major historical figures as it moves back half a century to analyse the impact of haemophilia and its role in shaping the turbulent politics, alongside the making and breaking of nations, which occurred during the first half of the twentieth century. Again in testing the viability of these various explanations the reader is invited to use the tests of credibility, likelihood, and verifiability in search of a realistic answer.

The next chapters of the book open out its exploration to consider types of history and approaches to it that historians have used, so that the interested reader can more readily engage with them. The first looks at how we might reconstruct the mental world of individuals who lived in the past, together with the idea of history and memory. We initially look at an example of a mental world created by an individual in the sixteenth century. This is a world manifestly different from our own, but we can see how a historian investigated this world through the imaginative use of sources. At its heart this particular project was intent on bringing this mental world to the attention of twentieth-century readers so they might readily appreciate the difference between the two. This idea is further reinforced by an examination of the history of death, where we encounter a multitude of ways in which individuals and institutions in the past created, portrayed, and managed death and its aftermath. The chapter also emphasizes how we might read these different creations and contrast them with each other, and particularly with our own attitude to this universal phenomenon – one that after all is central to human existence. After this, the chapter looks at how memories are themselves loaded with historical meaning through the ideas that they convey. By investigating inscriptions left on monuments and the nature of monuments themselves, we find they are able to tell us about the memories society wished to bequeath to the future. We also note, as we go through these inscriptions, that memories are contested and tell different versions of history that, in some cases, we already (perhaps mistakenly) thought we knew.

After this, the book moves from historical events to look at the secret history of ordinary things. This introduces the reader to aspects of social and cultural history, but also how that can interweave with other areas of history such as economic history and even political history. It showcases how examining the history of an apparently mundane phenomenon can reach outwards to encompass the history of many different areas of life. This chapter also reminds the reader that not all history is based on events, and that recapturing how material objects and material culture were generated within the past can provide important insights into that past. One dimension of this appreciation is the awareness of the idea of public history and heritage (as the driving mission of some historians), and this last suggestion is an important idea conveyed by this chapter.

The sixth chapter looks at the phenomenon of how history can become changed. That is, it shows why history is not definitive and can be superseded by subsequent interpretation. To do this we look at how the humanitarian explanation of how Britain came to end the slave trade was superseded by one which identified a seemingly more cynical reason for this occurrence. We also look at how historical explanations are sometimes used to predict the future, and how criticism of this assumption warns the historian about the limits of history and its connection with both the present and the future. Likewise, it also demonstrates how the implications of historical explanation are sometimes used by those without historical awareness, occasionally to the clear detriment of the society they live in.

Our last chapter does its best to bring all that we have learned together in a 'worked' example whereby we can see issues around sources, causality, theory, methods, and approaches played out. The example used here is the history of witchcraft, which demonstrates a whole range of methodologies, techniques, and varieties of history in the search to provide an explanation for and analysis of this unusual episode in European and American history between 1450 and 1750. Within this, the reader should be able to see all of the aspects discussed earlier in the book in action. Therefore this final 'worked' example ought to encourage the reader to commence making their own use of these aspects to investigate their own episodes of historical interest.

This final chapter is followed by a selection of further reading which outlines places where the interested reader can follow up in more depth some of the areas discussed in the course of this book. As with any selection of further reading, this cannot be comprehensive, but hopefully provides useful jumping-off points into the areas that have been discussed. Likewise the bibliographies and footnotes of these books should also be consulted for still deeper investigation.

Thus we now move through a number of examples of history's subject matters, its concerns, its approaches, and its perspectives. These stories and examples are easy to follow and think about, and it is always possible to reread these and contemplate them further aided by the additional material highlighted in the further reading section. History is always, and should always be, a fascinating voyage of discovery and realization. I hope many of you will have such moments during the course of this book – good luck and please enjoy yourselves!

2

History in context – finding and working with historical sources, falling in love and faking it

So now it is time for the reader to be introduced to the very first of the examples spread liberally throughout this book. This one in particular introduces us to historical sources and their relationship to some ideas we have already met. By investigating a whole area of historical study it becomes possible to encounter and explore simultaneously the range of historical approaches, the variety of sources that a historian might use to produce an explanation, and the different techniques that can be brought to bear on a historical subject or problem.

Although, as we may have discovered, historians have their own preconceptions and approaches, it remains an inescapable fact that the history they are investigating and eventually hope to write cannot be done without historical sources. History literally depends on the existence of historical sources, otherwise there is no evidence on which to base any history at all. Sometimes the historical context of the history we are investigating has an important bearing on the sources we use and what they might be saying to us. In ancient societies it is often the case that portable examples of writing (for example, the ancient equivalent of paper) are far less likely to survive than the writing preserved on stone tombstones and monuments. Indeed, much of what we know about the Roman world and day-to-day life within it is conveyed by the information on tombstones. However, as with any source, we must be prepared to consider the original function of tombstones, because the writing on these was commemorating someone's life and, equally, this took considerable time to engrave and carve. So we must remember that the words we read now were the product of a great deal of thought and were likewise invested with an importance to speak to subsequent generations. These are often grandiose pronouncements, far removed from a hastily constructed shopping list which takes considerably less thought to construct. Thus historians of Rome have a relative abundance of tombstone texts and would actively crave the chance to look at more mundane texts like shopping lists. This is precisely why archaeologists were so excited when they found such shopping lists whilst excavating the Northumbrian fort on Hadrian's Wall called Vindolanda. This told a much more ordinary (and more fascinating) story about everyday life in ancient Rome that they had not known up to this point, and a story that they could not have learned from a string of tombstone obituaries.

In a similar manner, historians have very little to work with if they want to investigate what Roman emperors thought of themselves, their power, and their capacity to rule. Although we do have histories of their reigns written by other commentators, these do not necessarily give us a direct insight into the precise personality of the emperor involved. Besides, historical accounts of this written by others may have bias and are simply not the same as directly encountering the views of emperors themselves. So how could we at this distance possibly hope to encounter what Roman emperors actually thought of themselves? This is where historians demonstrate their ingenuity with historical sources, since a number of them have looked at Roman coins and their depiction of these emperors as pictures of what these men (and very occasionally women) thought of themselves and their power. On these we can see symbols linking them with gods, with specific parts of the empire, and with messages they wanted to convey to their imperial subjects in depictions of imperial cities and recent battles won. Coins are also a good way of tracing the history of many usurpers who claimed to be the new emperor and frantically claimed legitimacy by striking coins with their image on them, to be circulated amongst their probably bemused subjects. Having used ingenuity to uncover evidence from an unlikely potential source, it is then, of course, the job of the historian to interpret this evidence.

The history of love: sources and their context

Human emotional relationships are one of the most universal experiences – so how would historians bring to bear techniques, perspectives, and sources to investigate this phenomenon? A historian might choose to produce a wide, expansive history which explored love, sex, and marriage since the earliest times up to the present. It is an interesting question whether such a long-term history would provide evidence of progress in the area of human relationships. This would largely be because it is probably true to say that one of the most likely findings would be that experiences have been so diverse that it would be difficult to be definitive. Nonetheless, such a history would describe the success of many human relationships in the past as some demonstration of human achievement. In making a value judgement a historian might hope that one aspect of progress entailed the transition from arranged, dynastic, and economically motivated marriage (to produce offspring) to a model of affectionate companionate marriage. However, they would also have to note that this is certainly not the norm in every culture and our original thought betrays a particularly Western bias. Likewise this cannot simply be portrayed as somehow definitively 'modern'. If the historian wanted to investigate the nature of love and romance in the remote past, he or she would be faced with a need to be ingenious with the historical sources they would use. Once again, the survival of such sources causes problems for the historian. Quite often when looking at subjects that do not leave as concrete a record as kingship or government, it can be useful to draw on literary evidence. This will of course have survived because the original text will be copied and reprinted many times right through to the modern period.

Looking at love and marriage in the medieval and early modern world might involve having to look creatively at the literature of the period as much as at any scattered historical sources that might remain. The works of Geoffrey Chaucer might tell us much about the variety of human experience associated with medieval love, sex, and marriage. The *Miller's Tale* tells us about a bawdy world of unrestrained sexuality and reminds us of the longevity of the association between sex, bodily functions, and humour. Meanwhile the *Merchant's Tale* discusses the age-old problems associated with the marriage of a young woman to a much older man and how he is cuckolded (betrayed) by her handsome younger suitor. This also tells much about how, even in medieval times, there was a discrepancy between 'arranged' unions and those based on emotional or sexual preference. We also gain an insight into the sexuality of medieval women through the Wife of Bath who readily informs us that she has no desire to live her life as a virgin or unmarried widow, nor does her reading of the Bible instruct her to do so. She gives us a full picture of her carnal appetites, and even discloses that she was unable to restrain herself from 'eyeing up' the man who became her next husband at the funeral of her previous one!

The medieval view of love might be approachable through sources related to the so-called 'courtly love' tradition, in which love is associated with the suffering of being unfulfilled or unrequited and often illicit. This is evident in one of the most celebrated romance stories of the period, Thomas Mallory's *Mort d'Arthur*, which is our leading historical source for the stories associated with King Arthur. Whether they tell us anything about the supposedly real King Arthur is debateable but, importantly, they nonetheless tell us much about medieval society's expectations in the area of love and relationships. In this work, Lancelot is forced by the code of courtly love to 'worship' Queen Guinevere from afar. His forbearance at this unrequited love is held up as a major theme associated with the chivalry of the period and used to define the medieval masculine attitude to love. He is prepared to defend her good name and fight for her, honour associating his manly bravery and strength with the depth of his love for the queen. At one point, in an exceptionally masculine view of love, he suggests the depth of his emotional feelings for Guinevere will enable him to bend the bars of the prison allowing him to enter her cell. These of course are duly bent aside by his passion, with little apparent problem. However, Lancelot and Queen Guinevere do eventually consummate their love behind King Arthur's back, leading to the enduring theme of guilt and betrayal.

Other medieval romances have similar themes, enabling the historian to see common patterns as well as variations. The romance *Guy of Warwick*, composed around 1300, has the central character fall in love with the daughter of the Earl of Warwick who rejects him because he is not of knightly status, demanding that he prove himself. He comes back to her having been made a knight, but, infuriatingly for Guy of Warwick, still falls short – for now she demands that he be nothing less than the finest knight in the world. After this the bulk of the story involves a great number of adventures through Europe, which encompass imprisonment, meetings with Saracens, successful fights with giants, and an eventual return to his ladylove. Unfortunately in this epic he dies before they can become a couple and their love remains unrequited. Already we might speculate how this tells us about the themes of love, loss, and longing in the medieval world. However, it is always worth looking out for other things such sources might be telling us. Both these stories involve the creation of extremes of masculinity in which men are expected to do brave and chivalric deeds as a means of winning the approval and love of women. Thus, we are starting to see one of the cultural conventions that made medieval warfare and episodes like the Crusades not simply possible, but also actively desirable for men wanting to live up to an ideal.

The world of Shakespeare similarly portrays differing experiences of love and human relationships. *Hamlet* shows a tortured man and his distracted love for Ophelia – a woman who arguably loses her mind because her paramour does not pay her enough attention. Beatrice and Benedick in *Much Ado About Nothing* portray a courting couple as a jousting meeting of intellectual equals. *Romeo and Juliet* is a forceful reminder of how love was not always approved of when it crossed social boundaries of whatever kind. The two central characters in *The Taming of the Shrew*, Petruchio and Katherine, show us an insight into the early modern world's 'discourses' about obedience and rebellion within marriage. Even Macbeth and Lady Macbeth show us a husband and wife working as a team to achieve shared goals, however despicable, ambitious, and wrong-headed. The love of Anthony for Cleopatra also suggests to us issues that occur when love is mixed with matters of state and two individuals have to cross cultures. Other writers, contemporary with Shakespeare, of what became known as 'revenge tragedy' saw love as a component part of a heady cocktail that also contained jealousy, envy, violence, and death. Generally these individuals located the actions of their dramas in contemporary Italy, also telling us much about how Protestant Elizabethan England viewed its Catholic enemies and rivals on the continent of Europe. Although obviously not about romantic love, the family squabbles experienced by King Lear and his daughters Regan, Goneril, and Cordelia, alongside the subplot involving the illegitimate son of the Duke of Gloucester, Edmund, all investigate themes of unconditional love, jealousy, resentment, and rejection within the family unit. Looking at these public depictions of men and women and their relationships would also persuade the historian to ask the question just how influential they might have been to subsequent couples in these centuries and beyond. A cultural historian would thus be very interested in how each generation learned to think about the idea of marriage and relationships, and how these are shaped and informed by both a popular and wider culture. This might profitably be charted by looking at changing emphases and interpretations within productions of these plays in different historical periods. How, for example, would a pre-1960s production of *The Taming of the Shrew* be likely to consider the final scene where Katherine submits to Petruchio? How exactly would this compare to a post-1960s feminist production of the same play?

Moving on a century, a historian who wanted to investigate the attitudes of eighteenth-century individuals to pre-marital sex and its pitfalls might want to consult Samuel Richardson's *Pamela*, which tells the story of a servant maid who becomes the target of her master's affection. His elevated social station prevents him from proposing marriage so he appears only interested in pre-marital sex. Pamela continually rejects him even though he resorts to imprisoning her. Eventually his lust turns to love and he casts aside his concerns about her lowly origin and he proposes marriage – a venture confirmed as a success by a similarly successful sequel to the book. This work tells us simultaneously about social standing and marriage as well as about the difference between this and casual sex in the eighteenth century. However, it can also be read as a manual for women seeking to gain the heart of an overenthusiastic suitor, initially only interested in a brief sexual liaison. Likewise it can be read as a manual for persuading men to pursue the ambition of love rather than sex.

Those in the eighteenth century who were thinking of embarking on marriage would find significant sources of guidance available. Expectations centring on marriage can be explored through looking at the numerous conduct books that existed during this period. These tell us much about the growth and development of manners as something driving social interaction and human relationships. These books were written to address men and women separately and conjured up an ideal of how each gender should behave – even sometimes giving a clear lead as to what each gender would find attractive in the other. This would shape the behaviour of the gender reading the book, whilst also shaping their expectations of how the other gender was supposed to behave. But history occasionally throws up some surprises about sources which can suddenly shine a light on an area we did not know about. When investigating eighteenth-century France and the use of conduct books within this society, the famous French historian Roger Chartier discovered that several sets of conduct books, which contained a series of model letters for individuals to copy and use, were selling in numbers ridiculously far beyond their target audience. He was reasonably certain that the individuals who could actually make use of the books aimed at the gentry were at most a few hundred. Yet these books were selling numbers significantly beyond this and this constituted something of a mystery. However, it was only when the structure of these books was looked at that the reason for this wider consumption became clear. These letters were listed in an order in which the young aristocratic man might use them. The early ones consisted of requests to visit and see a young woman who had supposedly caught the young man's eye. There then followed a model letter asking for the father's permission to court the young woman, and eventually a letter asking for her hand in marriage. There then followed letters which fulfilled certain needs related to the rites of passage associated with married life. What Chartier noticed was that, viewed from a distance, this was a story that described everything from first furtive glance to married life and that this wider audience were not using the books as a guide to conduct. Instead large numbers of people were reading them like a novel, in an age when the mainstream popular consumption of novels was still quite some distance away in time.

Again moving on a century, a historian might use personal journals and diaries as a way of investigating the thoughts and feelings of either the highest or lowest in the land. Queen Victoria's diaries have often been used by historians to undermine the view that the Victorians were sexually repressed and stuffy. Queen Victoria herself emerges as a woman with very strong sexual drives and her feelings for Prince Albert very clearly run the whole gamut of the physical and the emotional. In an age when large families were viewed as a virtue, Queen Victoria confided in her diary that her almost never-ending succession of pregnancies very obviously got in the way of her physical relationship with Prince Albert.

Occasionally even material about love and marriage can contain other messages. *The National Reformer*, a republican newspaper in England, was capable of providing advice to its readers about how they should choose a partner for marriage. This suggested the couple should agree about most things, have similar views about religion, and be approximately similar ages and appear virtuous. They should avoid being in debt and be economically solvent, and all such individuals contemplating marriage should not be closely related. In particular they should not marry first cousins who 'often have ill formed and insane children'. On the face of it the historian might ask what this advice is doing in a political paper. However, a closer look reveals that it is using the idea of good marriage as a code to undermine and attack the monarchy. During the previous decade Queen Victoria had more or less been a recluse after the death of her beloved Albert, emerging only to ask Parliament perpetually for expensive dowries for what seemed like an endless stream of daughters. She had failed to discharge her civic duties and had even been discovered misrepresenting the condition of her own finances in her quest for further parliamentary grants. *The National Reformer* and its marriage advice were alluding to this behaviour, but its ultimate and considered attack on the marriage of Queen Victoria was that she and Albert had been first cousins. Thus by setting up an ideal of marriage, the institution was used by Republicans in England as a political stick with which to beat the Victorian monarchy.

Social and economic historians might use their techniques to look at other aspects of love, marriage, and families. Using demographic (population) data across time and space would tell these researchers what the average age of marriage has been, how it has changed, when it has changed, and perhaps why it has changed. Things can be deduced from whether people make conscious decisions to marry early or late, how many children they choose to have, and how likely those children are to survive. Demographers also go further than this to look at the size, composition, and life cycle of individual family groups, and have even gone so far as to construct whole communities to show the web of inter-relationships and dependencies that exist within these.

However, as we are fully aware, love and marriage are not always plain sailing and it is possible to gain insights into the history of how and why relationships break down. For this purpose, legal records and court cases are the most obvious and fertile sources to use. From these we can trace the history of extramarital sex, of domestic violence, and other related themes such as the history of infanticide. Love and marriage are also an important area where communities give voice to their moral expectations and what they consider to be acceptable norms of behaviour. It is here that we encounter phenomena such as the famous skimmington ride, as portrayed in Thomas Hardy's *Mayor of Casterbridge.* In this, individuals known to the local community to be conducting an illicit affair were displayed and mocked by the local populace, sometimes in effigy and sometimes in person. Such communal expression was also used to punish both errant wives and husbands and sometimes to ridicule a man whose wife was known to be unfaithful to him. These incidents readily occurred in England between the seventeenth and the end of the nineteenth century, and the custom was transported to the American Colonies where it survived, particularly in the southern states, over a similar timespan.

The history of divorce and how laws about it are enacted is also useful for telling us about what a particular society thinks about the family and the relationships around which it is organized. At various times societies have sought to make divorce either harder or easier for individuals to obtain, and this too has its history. Likewise, sources and the phenomena they tell us about also persuade us that history has detailed stories to tell, beyond what a more apparently enlightened age may superficially think of them. One such story is that of wifesale. When the distinguished historian Edward Thompson began speaking about this topic at English universities, his presentations were lobbied by outraged feminists who saw in the title and the apparent subject an episode that degraded the image and status of women and their history. It was only when Thompson got into his stride that the truth emerged. Wifesale (even through its mere title) did seem to treat the woman as a commodity, since the man received some form of payment for the departure of his wife – something which, for all the world, looked like a grubby financial transaction with the woman treated merely as a chattel for sale. Yet this needed to be seen in its historical context since many lower-class marriages had an important economic element to them which enabled couples to live more cheaply than one, and to divide their tasks accordingly. In wifesale the man was being compensated for the loss of his wife's productive power within their relationship, which had been both economic and personal. However, this 'compensation' also gave a much wider clue to what was going on. Thompson had looked at local records and newspaper reports and these demonstrated that almost all of the wifesales he had investigated were in fact instituted by the woman herself. This meant that a wifesale was far more complex than the apparent degradation of a woman – but was instead an assertion of her independence and of her active and conscious wish to choose another life partner. In effect, it was a working-class method of getting divorced when the legal equivalent was prohibitively expensive and in practice unavailable.

Love and marriage would also provide the opportunity for individual historians to bring to bear the fruits of their engagement with various species of theory. We mentioned earlier how conduct books reflected the cultivation of manners, and certainly historians who believe in ideas associated with progress might seek to describe the growth of the regulated behaviour of individuals over time as evidence of such progress. However, as is always the case, such views have a polar opposite, in this case in Michel Foucault's ideas about sexuality and its history. Foucault believed the history of human relationships and sex had not been about affection or desire, but instead it had been about the exercise of power by individuals over themselves and other individuals. Sex, so Foucault argued, had become an area for the application of specialist knowledge to impose control, as was the case with other areas like punishment or the workings of the human mind studied through psychiatry. These forms of knowledge were a cause of suspicion for Foucault, who saw them as controlling influences that ultimately limited human freedom.

Historians who wanted to look at such power in relationships expressed through language and discourses, alongside the history of their impacts, could investigate the cult of the romantic popular novel from the eighteenth century onwards. Likewise, the portrayal of marriage in everything from Hollywood films to daily television soap operas. The spectacular growth and consumption of print media during the twentieth century has also produced a great number of sources for investigating this subject. It is possible for example to look at how some southern European societies were changing in the years after the Second World War. By looking at magazines, their fictional stories, and their problem pages, it is possible to see how Italian women in the 1950s came to expect careers and an equal partnership with their lovers and husbands – an independence scarcely imaginable even ten years earlier. In this instance what is interesting for the historian is to think about how far these sources might reflect this change, but equally how far they might have been actively influencing it – both have a potential history here.

Lastly we should mention how the concerns of history and even the subject of history changes in response to the perspectives of the society that writes that history. Thus one of the newer areas of investigation within the subject of love and emotion has been the writing of history about same-sex relationships. Just as previous minorities have been hidden from history, lesbian, gay, and bisexual history is in the process of being recovered where it had previously been ignored or simply marginalized. History always marches on, and the proof of this will be in the obvious need for a historian reading this book some time in the future to add important paragraphs to update its account of the history of love and relationships. To do this will require a new look at existing sources or a successful search for new ones.

How to change history with sources: fact and fiction

It is probably the dream of everyone who reads and writes history to uncover and discover something no one else knows about. Everyone who has the slightest interest in history wants to be the person who is credited with finding the truth about an historical event. Historians who work in archives and libraries also fantasize about discovering an unknown historical source that potentially changes everything we know about a particular topic. The hope that suddenly we will find something miraculous hidden in the archive has driven generations of historians onwards in their search to explain the past.

This phenomenon teaches us two important things. Firstly, history and its creation rely implicitly on what historical sources can tell us. They are literally the raw material of history and without them the task of the historian is almost impossible. Sources convey to the historian everything about the past, from facts and details to impression and bias, and it is only from these that the whole picture of what happened in history can be drawn. Although for most of its existence history meant the record of what had been written down, this picture has changed somewhat since the second half of the twentieth century when objects, buildings, and even the landscape itself began to be considered as historical sources in their own right. Each of these, so it was suggested, could be read in exactly the same manner as a historical document. A field, for instance, could show evidence of Iron Age occupation which had been overlaid by evidence of a Roman fort or villa. This in turn might have been overlaid by the evidence of the eighteenth-century obsession with field enclosure, and then by twentieth-century housing. Secondly, primary sources and their discovery are also important ways of reminding ourselves that history is still being written. The power of primary sources, when placed alongside one another to tell us a new story, is the means by which history evolves and alters our understanding of the past.

Certainly the discovery of new historical sources that give historians the occasional 'Eureka moment' are few and far between, but occasionally this does happen. When it does, it is very important to keep a sense of proportion and to ensure that the historian uses their critical skills sensibly and for the benefit of the subject. Indeed any historian should exercise a checklist whereby sources are tested against measures of credibility, likelihood, and verifiability. Firstly, credibility: do the sources themselves seem credible and believable on their own terms, and are they likely to have been produced for specific and credible purposes? Does the story they tell seem possible given what else we know about the subject involved? Secondly, likelihood: is it likely such a source is genuine and can we verify this? Lastly, verifiability: do we have mechanisms to check what is being said by the source? Can its account be compared with others or can we find other sources to enable us to fit our source into a pattern or series, together with evidence from elsewhere, to corroborate the apparently new story being told?

It is particularly important to think about how the new story fits into the big picture of the known historical record. In other words, how much does this new source really alter what we know about a particular historical topic or subject? Is it really capable of altering large swathes of history or is it in fact altering only a smaller part of this? In making this evaluation we are making decisions about just how powerful historical sources actually are, in terms of the history they will help write. However, we must be clear about two fundamentally important things. Firstly, are our sources going to pass our tests of credibility, likelihood, and verifiability, and secondly, even if we are going to allow new sources to produce a new account of a historical event or period, how much of the conventional story does it really change?

To demonstrate this I have chosen to use two fabricated pieces of historical evidence to demonstrate how new information can potentially change the interpretation of a specific historical event. At first sight it may seem strange to choose false pieces of evidence to demonstrate how evidence can change history – after all, enough genuine pieces of evidence have done precisely that. However, choosing false evidence that did *not* alter history serves two very useful purposes for the reader. Firstly, it allows the possibility of easily obtaining and reading the generally accepted or 'true' account of events. It is then easy to compare this 'true' account with the one produced by the use of false evidence to see how they are different. The use of some 'false' evidence also highlights further the dangers of historians striving too hard to change the 'true' account of history, and serves as an important warning about allowing enthusiasm to supplant method and reason. As we have discussed, all historical sources that will be used to construct an explanation should have been subjected to our tests of credibility, likelihood, and verifiability. I have chosen two examples roughly six hundred years apart. Both of these stories had generally accepted versions of the truth until they appeared to have been challenged by the emergence of new historical sources. To ensure that our approach to these stories is not coloured by scholarly bias or the power of past historical opinion, it is important to remember that both of the newly discovered sources described here are generally considered to be forgeries.

Edward II: violently murdered or died peacefully in his bed?

It is probably an extremely safe bet to say that King Edward II was one of the most unpopular monarchs to have sat on the English throne – but then he had an extremely hard act to follow. His father Edward I (the King depicted in the film *Braveheart*) had been the so-called 'Hammer of the Scots' and had also extended the influence of the English throne deep into the heartland of Wales. As part of his peace treaty with the Welsh, Edward I had been asked to provide the Welsh nation with a prince born in Wales. Edward had duly obliged by hastily arranging for his pregnant wife to be moved to a castle in Wales. When she fortunately gave birth to her son, Edward I presented the child to the Welsh nobility as the prince born in Wales they had asked for. This episode founded the office of Prince of Wales, which is still part of England's monarchical system – but is also probably the first joke widely remembered in English history.

However, as time went on Edward I might have considered that the ultimate joke had been played upon him by fate and circumstances. This son, later to become King Edward II, was significantly poor raw material for a future king. He showed no interest or aptitude for the duties required of a king and instead was more interested in the unkingly pursuits of swimming, rowing, and shoeing horses. Likewise, he did not inherit his father's determination or strength of character when it came to matters of state. When Edward II became king, things went rapidly from bad to worse. He was responsible for the catastrophic defeat at the battle of Bannockburn which dealt a near-fatal blow to the English Crown's attempts to control its unruly northern Scottish neighbour. Edward was also considered to have especially poor taste in advisers, which created further problems in the wider kingdom. The first of these was a knight called Piers Gaveston who became hated because he was the king's favourite, but also because he was a foreigner from the French province of Poitou. It was also rumoured at the time, and many subsequent chroniclers, historians, and playwrights have sought to confirm, that Edward II was a homosexual and that this was the true nature of his relationship with Gaveston. Both the hatred of Gaveston and the later military defeat brought the nobility close to rebellion which eventually broke out. In 1312 a group of nobles captured Gaveston and hurriedly executed him, stimulating anger and distress in equal measure in the mind of Edward II.

The king did not learn any significant lessons from his reliance on court favourites and later in his reign he also adopted another nobleman, Hugh Despenser, again with unfortunate results. The power and patronage of the Despenser family made dangerous and influential enemies in the kingdom. Perhaps chief among these was the king's wife Queen Isabella of France who by this time had taken a lover, another nobleman called Roger Mortimer. The queen fled to France where she managed to raise an army which had the explicit intention of defeating and overthrowing her husband King Edward II. By now the king had lost support in almost every sector of society and was left with only the support of the Despenser family when he was captured in October 1326. Although England had no good precedent for getting rid of a bad king, Queen Isabella and Roger Mortimer persuaded the nobles in parliament, the bishops, and the London crowd to accept the removal of the king. The king eventually struck a bargain that he would abdicate the throne if his son were allowed to succeed him, bringing his intensely troubled reign to an end.

However, a deposed king remained something of an inconvenience and he subsequently disappeared from view. Whatever happened to Edward clearly happened in secret and away from prying eyes. Most historians have accepted the standard explanation of what became of Edward. He was imprisoned for some considerable time at Berkeley Castle in Gloucestershire whilst the new regime decided what to do with him. During this time he proved something of a dangerous nuisance, since there were at least two attempts to rescue him, with one of them enabling him to escape as far as Oxford. Some suggest that there was a concerted attempt to starve him to death, to which he was annoyingly resistant. However, most agree that a decision was made to end his life, either by Mortimer and Isabella or by nobles acting on their own initiative. It is generally agreed by most historians that Edward was very probably killed on, or just before, 28 September 1327. Yet there are two versions of precisely how he died. Some believe he was suffocated by three men; John Mautravers, Thomas Gourney, and the King's gaoler. A more colourful chronicler's account suggests that two of these men held the king down whilst the third inserted a red-hot iron roasting spit into his anus. According to this story the idea was simultaneously to rebuke him for his homosexuality and to ensure his manner of death left no marks on his body. Either way no one disputed the fact that Edward had died when this event was announced on 28 September 1327. Some credence was lent to the story of a treacherous murder by the fact that Edward II's sarcophagus was the first of any medieval English king to have completely covered the body and hidden it from view. This also, of course, led to speculation that the corpse buried was not Edward, or indeed that the sarcophagus did not contain a body at all.

This was the orthodox story of the death of Edward II and it has been generally accepted by experts of the medieval period right up until this day. However, this version of what happened to Edward was questioned in the nineteenth century when a French scholar chanced upon a most surprising letter hidden in an Italian archive. This letter claimed to be the 'Confession of Edward II' which also detailed his life after his so-called death in 1327. According to this letter, which had been written by an Italian bishop, Manuelle de Fieschi, Edward had escaped to Ireland but he was eventually able to reach the continent of Europe. The letter stated that he was received by the Pope at Avignon before travelling further through France and Germany. At the time the Italian Bishop of Vercelli was writing this supposed confession, the individual believed to be the surviving Edward II was living as a hermit in northern Italy.

Although different writers, intrigued by the allure of a cover-up and the desire to uncover something unknown, have tried to investigate the truth of this story, most professional historians dismiss this as a forgery or a story concocted for gain. As we have said, this version of what happened to Edward is based on a document that is a forgery. We already have a generally accepted account of his fate – the murder in Berkeley Castle. However, we can now fruitfully compare versions and assess how the truth of Edward's escape to Italy would alter the course of history if it actually had any basis in fact – if it were to pass the tests of credibility, likelihood, and verifiability. Certainly it would give us a supposedly new 'truth' about what precisely happened to this much maligned King of England. But would it really alter our much wider and deeper picture of medieval England and its history? We have to conclude that it really would not, and our clues to this lie in the nature of the fake/forgery story itself. The Edward who supposedly escaped from Berkeley Castle clearly went to ground with the intention of merely surviving and continuing his life in comparative obscurity. He did not lobby to regain the throne. He did not raise a foreign army of mercenaries to retake it by force, nor did he try to petition his relatives or his son to allow him back into England. If the 'Confession of Edward II' were true then this wronged King of England decided to live out his days quietly and to devote himself to religious contemplation – possibly to atone for his past selfishness, neglect of duty, and indifference to the plight of his own kingdom. Thus the truth of the 'Confession of Edward II' really does not alter our big picture of medieval England and its political history. Irrespective of whether the letter is true or not, its contents would not alter what happened to the medieval England of Edward's day. His son Edward III still ascended the throne unmolested and, at least in the early part of his reign, restored order to the kingdom, leading it into a new period of prosperity.

Thus this source, the counterfeit 'Confession of Edward II', would not fundamentally alter the shape of medieval English history as we know it, even if it were true. This is because its contents do not have a significant impact on the major political events. Even if the king survived he did nothing to meddle in politics ever again and the story is merely one of human interest. Thus, by ensuring we keep our mind on the significance of the source, we can determine whether it alters our big picture of history or not.

Hitler's diaries: a pointless scam or an important insight into the psychology of the Holocaust?

In April 1983 the historical world was stunned by the revelations emanating from the German magazine *Stern*. According to its front cover the hitherto unknown diaries of Adolf Hitler had been discovered. The magazine had been able to get hold of them, and was ready to print excerpts for an unsuspecting, but nonetheless excited world. These diaries had apparently been flown out of Berlin at the end of the war, only for the plane carrying them to have been shot down near Dresden in Eastern Germany. From here, these documents had been in the safekeeping of an East German army general. Through intermediaries, acting on behalf of cautious and necessarily secretive individuals, the story and the diaries were brought to the West by the *Stern* reporter Gerd Heidemann, who had for many years nurtured an almost obsessive interest in the Nazi period and its memorabilia. He convinced his magazine not only that the diaries were genuine but that it should rapidly delve into its own pocket to acquire them before other newspapers did so. Only then could it guarantee that it had exclusive access to the historical scoop of the twentieth century.

Although there was wonder and scepticism in relatively equal measure, *Stern* magazine and Gerd Heidemann, having committed their reputations and in the case of the magazine considerable funds to the venture, proceeded frantically to convince themselves of the authenticity of the diaries. The route to establishing this authenticity involved handwriting experts and the opinion of some expert historians. The most notable of these was Hugh Trevor-Roper who, although primarily an expert on the sixteenth and seventeenth century, had actually been involved in working for British intelligence at the end of the war, tracing Nazi survivors and refuting the stories that Hitler had somehow survived the bunker. Although initially sceptical, Trevor-Roper eventually became the most high-profile expert prepared to suggest that the diaries were genuine.

Stern intended to launch these on an expectant world at a major press conference. However, at this event some very pertinent and damaging questions were asked by a number of reporters which left the magazine staff considerably ill at ease and red-faced. Why had *Stern* failed to offer a cast-iron guarantee about the authenticity of the diaries? Why had they failed to use forensic testing on the ink used? And what of the obviously fake letter heads of other material included with the diaries? The only solution to the quandary *Stern* had got itself into was to seek further expert evidence that would show the diaries to be genuine beyond question. Thus this process went beyond the skills of historians and handwriting experts to forensic scientists who would actually probe the physical composition of the diaries. Their conclusions shocked *Stern* magazine but scarcely surprised those who had been sceptical at the press conference. The diaries themselves, which physically looked like stained and damaged ledger books, were actually of post-war origin. Chemical analysis of the ink used also showed this to have been manufactured after 1945 and had not been on the paper for as many years as would have been essential for the diaries to be authentic. Thereafter the saga of the Hitler diaries degenerated into a sorry scandal with regret, recrimination, and some very tarnished reputations. After the fraud was uncovered Gerd Heidemann and the perpetrator of the whole scam, a forger named Konrad Kujau (whom Heidemann had passed off as the East German general), were both sentenced to significant prison terms.

Although forensic science was able to tell us the truth about the authenticity of the Hitler diaries, what surprises us now is that historians seemed quite unable to detect a fraudulent source when they saw one. Although any historian will agree that hindsight is an easy phenomenon to indulge when thinking about history, it has a very useful purpose in this instance. Looking backwards at the history contained in the Hitler diaries, it is possible to see how historically worthless they really were. Those who initially looked at the contents of them marvelled at the simplicity and ordinariness of some of the entries. Hitler apparently noted his engagements day-by-day and also recorded numerous dull and uninspiring comments about his health and his relationship with Eva Braun. At the time many, laughingly, saw this as apparent proof of the authenticity of the diaries. The fact that world-shattering events rubbed shoulders with domestic trivia tipped the balance for minds that already wished to be convinced.

However, delving deeper reveals still more damning flaws in the way some members of the historical profession approached their task. An overview of the diaries did not tell us a single new thing about Hitler, his behaviour, or the history of the Nazi period. It is now well established that all of the historical material that appeared within the Hitler diaries was available in a variety of published accounts, and this was quite apart from some glaring inaccuracies that equally should have been spotted at the time. Now this might, at first sight, suggest that the diaries corroborated everything we knew they ought to have done. However, this should have created a sense of unease amongst those concerned at a considerably earlier stage of proceedings than actually happened. These diaries created a Hitler character that had emerged unaltered from textbook accounts of the Third Reich. Many individuals had also quite forgotten that Hitler had a reputation for disliking the chore of handwriting his instructions and orders, preferring to delegate this to others.

Although trumpeted, and leaving a considerable dent in the pocket of *Stern* magazine, the Hitler diaries startlingly told us nothing that we did not already know. Thus they were of considerably less value historically than the 'Confession of Edward II' which at least attempted to tell us a different story about false death and subsequent life of this medieval monarch. Nonetheless both of these supposed historical sources were fakes and thus add little to the historical record, except possibly telling us a little about the history of forgers and forgery!

But there remain two important things to consider about the history of the Hitler diaries and the insight they provide into human nature when faced with the historically significant. So many individuals, many who should really have known better, were anxious to believe that they had found and were staring at the Hitler diaries. The pressure to believe that they were authentic became overwhelming and almost mutated into an article of faith. If mankind had found the Hitler diaries, then the answer to so many questions would flow from this remarkable discovery. In this frenzy too many people did not keep their feet on the ground and scrutinize the historical content more carefully. Most worryingly the desire to stare at the Hitler diaries, irrespective of their content, took us away from history and towards the collection of memorabilia.

In a sense this does take us back to the points raised earlier in this chapter and sounds an important warning to those who uncover a new historical source. The excitement and wish to be the person with a historically important finding must be resisted until after the duties of the serious historian have been performed. This also persuades us still more firmly of the important questions a historian should ask of any primary source. Firstly, is it genuine? If it is, what does it do to alter our picture of history? The Hitler diaries manifestly fail both of these tests. The 'Confession of Edward II', whilst still almost certainly a forgery, does not significantly alter our picture of fourteenth-century English monarchical politics, even if it is a new story.

So what would a dramatic, history-altering document really look like? Once again it is tempting to go back to the Hitler diaries and to fantasize about what they might contain if we were to find a real set of them! Firstly, it is easy to construct a wish list, but it is worth remembering any such wish list is going to contain the details of things we really want to know about an historical figure or event. This is a research agenda that historians always hope can be answered by looking at new sources. The trouble with this is that all historians will potentially have their own wish list of what the 'diaries' ought to contain. Whilst all historians want to know the truth, most historians also want to see individual theories vindicated or disproved.

If we could find the real Hitler diaries (although this remains extremely unlikely) they could possibly contain a wealth of already known trivial information, or unknown material about which we could reasonably have made an educated guess. But there remain bigger historical questions to which we would want more definitive and convincing answers. The desire to gain access to such sources is something that should persuade historians to generate and ask more penetrating research questions. Historians would sit and hope that these diaries would tell us about Hitler's precise role in the Holocaust – was he its progenitor or did he endorse policy originated and promoted by others? The diaries might also tell us about Hitler's command decisions and how these were arrived at – decisions that conceivably altered the course of the war. We would also potentially gain insight into Hitler's state of mind and how this influenced the course of history. We may also learn more about his relationships with his commanders and his general staff. What did Hitler think of his allies, whether active in support of the war (like Mussolini in Italy) or more passive (like Franco in Spain)? Did Hitler ever confide to his diary doubts about his personal mission or doubts that he and Germany would win the war? What did he think of Rudolf Hess and his plan to collaborate with Britain? What were his plans for a post-war Germany triumphant against its enemies? All of these are questions that the whole historical world might hope that the discovery of the Hitler diaries might answer. It is also worth remembering that historians also have their own perspectives that they wish to see confirmed, particularly about such an emotive figure as Adolf Hitler. Those who see him as the architect of Europe's potential descent into darkness would obviously seek confirmation of this in the Hitler diaries. Similarly Holocaust deniers would crave a version of the diaries that either does not mention action against the Jews or a version which seeks to exonerate Hitler from blame and culpability.

Through this exploration of sources we have learned that the source is the starting point for all historical investigation and endeavours. However, we need to be cautious with sources since they need to be treated with sobriety and clear-headed appraisal. Occasionally they tell us important new things about history but they have to be subjected to considered judgement and evaluation – there are no Eureka moments in historical study. Instead they are replaced by more satisfactory, if more gradual, glows of realization.

Lastly, this should make everyone interested in history turn around and look back at what we feel confident that we *do* know. Previously established facts, based on work with verified sources, remain just that and we should be grateful for this. Scholarship and tests of evidence have made these into orthodoxy through the reasoned (non-Eureka-moment) work of generations of researchers. These painstaking workers have accepted that continued perspiration is the far more usual experience of the historian than sudden inspiration.

3

The search for 'truth' – establishing the facts, causes, and explanations

The assassination of John F. Kennedy

On 22 November 1963 the president of the USA, John F. Kennedy, was assassinated whilst visiting the city of Dallas, Texas. He was shot at approximately 3 PM, in the presence of his wife and a number of his close aides and advisers, as he was travelling in a presidential motorcade.

It is a salutary comment that, in the final analysis, this is all we can know for absolute certain of what actually happened to John F. Kennedy on that fateful afternoon. Almost all those who have read this far will certainly be concerned that this explanation is not complete or in any way satisfying. It does not contain important information that we would want to establish as fact or explanation, something that would enable us to analyse the events of that day with greater precision and accuracy. The need for such undisputed facts and a desire for the truth is one of the very strongest reasons that human civilization has for wanting a sophisticated and developed conception of history. Without this, simply retelling the events risks making this account nothing more than an unsatisfactory story.

This search for the truth is fundamental to us in moulding our conception of how life and events are given order and made to have meaning. Thus truth, trust in the facts, and the power of interpretations are what often enable individuals to cope with the world and shape their conceptions of good and evil. History is a search for truth, even if it is sometimes approached from some very different and contrasting directions. What we perceive the truth to be (drawing on facts we know and the interpretation we favour) also shapes the narrative that we give to history. As a result, many of the ideas about history that shape our lives rest on the establishment of these facts and fundamental truths. The search for the truth, as von Ranke argued, fundamentally drives the need to give shape to history. The consequence of this is that a historian strives for the truth to ensure that the history they write has the correct shape and tells the correct story. Thus an individual history written by an individual historian seeks to portray their version of the truth as a combination of their ability to prove a series of facts and shape these into an interpretation.

To stick closely to our example of Kennedy's assassination, a definitive explanation of the truth is difficult to construct, so we must be wary of precisely which so-called facts and explanations are allowed to enter our story. This is because there is a vast range of competing stories of what occurred in Dallas that day in 1963. This really gets us, rapidly, to the heart of what it means to think about history and what it means to be a historian. This is because historians are always in search of what they argue is the truth – however threadbare it ends up becoming, or potentially illusory as the postmodernists of this book's introduction seek to argue. This suggests to us that the search for truth does have a fundamental function in how we perceive and use history, even if we decide the collection of 'discourses' is 'the truth'. This is in fact the key to this chapter – not necessarily that we can be assured that we will ultimately find 'truths', but that the 'search for truth' is something that binds all historians. Frequently, it is these different methods of searching that shape the truth that historians eventually 'discover'.

But first, why should we seek to go beyond the established facts as stated above – that paltry collection of agreed truths?

Surely to do so would involve risks of creating inaccuracies that are unacceptable in our search for truth? There are several related answers to this question, all of which compel us to provide an 'account' of what happened. Most importantly, the death of John F. Kennedy was a truly momentous event in American history. It is certain that other men died in Dallas during late November 1963 – but history (in its concern for those events that have the greatest impact on the world) tells us that it is Kennedy's death that should be considered important. As historians, we are therefore driven to start our investigation of what happened at this point. Put most simply, we do this by constructing hierarchies of facts, stories, and explanations. We must then decide the relative value and importance of these, and the way we place them alongside each other is what constructs our history. We must also here rely on our experience of the world as we know it, a process that the nineteenth-century philosopher and historian R.G. Collingwood defined as knowing the natural world and its laws as a means of deciding the probability of a likely explanation.

We may know many facts about the events of that day in Dallas, but we have to create a hierarchy of what these facts tell us about the story we are investigating. Some are meaningless and irrelevant and must simply be acknowledged in passing or discarded. What the protagonists in Dallas may have had for breakfast or the design of shoes they were wearing may make for an interesting element in a description of the events, but no one could realistically say that they were in any sense of real or lasting importance as regards JFK's assassination. Our more important facts are those from which conclusions can be drawn that are pertinent to the story for which we are searching. Some facts will only yield up their significance when related to others. Indeed it can be said that conclusions are built precisely by considering a number of relevant facts together. On their own, individual facts can easily be misleading. So to construct a complete picture, as many facts as possible are needed to reach a conclusion. And even then, historians are always searching for more facts that might help shed new light on previous facts and interpretations.

We also have to deal with issues about what to do with the evidence that does exist and how this, in itself, can persuade us to ask probing questions. One of the central reasons that the assassination of John F. Kennedy has sparked so many questions is because the conventional, supposedly orthodox and official, explanation seems so incomplete and unsatisfactory. Indeed it is worth considering just how much the search for the truth is inspired by the inadequacy or failure of many official accounts of events. Most people consider the official investigation into Kennedy's assassination, known as the Warren Commission, to have heard its evidence and reached its verdict in something of a ridiculous and unnecessary hurry. Its conclusions seemed destined to fuel conspiracy theories although, paradoxically, its findings intended to close down speculation about an uncomfortable and nationally traumatic event. It concluded that the assassin they arrested for the crime, Lee Harvey Oswald, had acted alone. However, the Warren Commission is also known, notoriously, to have held back some evidence and material from the public gaze. Even years later, when freedom of information legislation would normally have made the disclosure of such documentation mandatory, files were released with a considerable number of blank pages where material had been censored or removed. This has inevitably fuelled the search for alternative explanations, which have taken on an ideological flavour of their own in their distrust of the American federal government.

Trading on concerns and fears about big and powerful government organizations conspiring against the ordinary American people, some explanations of the Kennedy assassination have entered the genre of conspiracy theory. Conspiracy theories have generally had an unwelcome place within most civilizations. In some respects it is possible to consider 'conspiracy theories' to be alternative histories. They are a particularly good example of an aspect of human psychology that in some people can dictate the history they are interested in and how this leads them to distort evidence to create a narrative with a particular bias. Conspiracy theories start from an assumption that the forces that shape a particular historical event or epoch are malevolent and evil, and they are also seen as seeking to shape the world through unacceptable, immoral, and uncivilized means.

Conspiracy theorists are ready (and almost always overeager) to lay blame and to consider that important events and actions have been covered up and hidden from view and scrutiny. This is seen to be at the will and intention of the supposedly dark forces controlling this particular historical event. The explanations are almost always elaborate and seem to specialize in the imaginative leap. They can start with a reasonable hypothesis but make much out of inference, coincidence, hearsay, and marginal evidence. This last facet of conspiracy theory is perhaps especially maddening for the historian because it means conspiracy theories cannot be refuted in the minds of their advocates, as there is no counter-evidence to refute a wayward idea, and hence sometimes they never seem to go away. The assassination of John F. Kennedy provides us with wonderful raw material for learning about how historians should properly sift information, work with explanations, and categorize theories and hypotheses to determine precisely how these might relate to the truth. When we investigate the assassination of John F. Kennedy, as we shall see, we encounter all grades of evidence, and almost all of them possess varying degrees of credibility, likelihood, and verifiability.

Many books have been written seeking to unpack a number of different conspiracy theories about who killed Kennedy and why. Even the briefest glance at the internet demonstrates that these conspiracy theories are numerous – one particular website suggests that there are no less than thirty-six of these – and, with the power of this particular medium of information retrieval and dispersal, they are quite liable to continue multiplying. With this bewildering array of possible explanations, it is no wonder that the American public craves the truth and is liable to be confused and lost when it tries to seek this. In sifting information we are unlikely to uncover what we consider to be the absolute truth about who killed John F. Kennedy, but our task as historians is to get as close to the truth as we can. So how do we do this? The first step is very clearly to rule out the explanations that appear far-fetched, incredible, and most unlikely. We do this by bringing to bear our own experience of life, which suggests to us what is likely to be true and what is not. In our own lives, when we interpret things that happen to us, we reach for the most likely explanation. These explanations themselves sometimes differ with the historical period and other contexts we live in. If we discover the laser printer in our office is not working, we will conclude it is a piece of machinery undergoing a mechanical fault. Thus we conclude we should call the engineer – an explanation that the laser printer is infected with evil spirits will seem manifestly less credible to us.

We must now seek to apply some of these insights from our own lived experience to this evidence as a means of getting closer to the truth of what happened to President Kennedy. We know that conspiracy theories about his death exist in wild abundance, but even within these we can discern hierarchies of facts and some which are more likely to pass our tests of credibility, likelihood, and verifiability. For example, one of the conspiracy theories is called 'the zero game' which asserts that since 1840 every American president that has been elected in a year ending with the digit zero has died in office. The claim is that the Kennedy assassination may have been arranged by some dark conspiracy which (according to taste and prejudice) implicates everyone from the freemasons, dissident Zionists, the Roman Catholic Church, to the British monarchy. It is true that this explanation does assemble some known facts, but its problem is that it selects poor ones and then makes a considerable leap of imagination rather than sensible probability. Very quickly we can dismiss much of this using our criteria of credibility, likelihood, and verifiability because there is simply no evidence that these deaths are anything other than coincidence. Ronald Reagan survived the curse of 'the zero game' and very clearly not all who did die in office were assassinated. Similarly there is no clear evidence (or past history) to suggest that the organizations mentioned have ever indulged in this kind of activity in recent times.

Our second step is to move up our hierarchy of explanations (again, using credibility, likelihood, and verifiability) to examine, in a little more detail, some of the suggested theories that are a shade more believable than theories that deal with mystic numbers. One theory suggests that the Israeli government, irritated by Kennedy's snooping into their nuclear weapons research programme, constructed the assassination under the guidance of President David Ben-Gurion. The only evidence we have to back this story up is the testimony of the Israeli dissident Mordechai Vanunu who testified to the West about Israel's nuclear programme in the 1980s. Interestingly Vanunu waited until 2004 to make his claim, and we might consider that his track record meant he was likely and willing to implicate the Israeli government in almost anything. At this point any historian must remind themselves that the actors in any historical event will have their own agendas and ulterior motives. This means that historians must be prepared to consider the bias of those who took part in historical events and particularly the bias of those who would have been involved in creating what has become historical evidence. Thus, in this instance, the bias of the witness detracts from the credibility of the testimony – in other words Vanunu does not offer objectivity to his explanation. We should also be prepared to look at the wider picture and note that there is no historical legacy of dislike and hatred between the state of Israel and successive US governments.

There is also a theory that considers the fatal shot which killed President Kennedy to have been fired by accident by a secret service agent who was travelling in the car behind. Whilst this theory suggests two other shots were fired by Lee Harvey Oswald, these were not the shots that killed Kennedy. The agent concerned was supposedly trying to respond to the shots fired by Oswald, but lost his balance in the confusion and accidentally discharged the third shot which killed the president. If this was the explanation, it seems odd that nobody else witnessed what had happened and had subsequently been prepared to come forward. Similarly, a simple accident would have had little need for a cover-up and, in the end, might have been one of the safest explanations to make the American people live with, since it would rule out the malevolence of individuals or foreign powers. Interestingly the agent implicated in this explanation, an individual named George Hickey, tried to sue Bonar Menninger, the author of the book who put forward this theory. Menninger claimed forensic evidence could prove the bullet came from Hickey's gun, but that the president's brother Robert Kennedy had authorized a cover-up to protect Hickey's unfortunate accident from scrutiny. Likewise Menninger suggested the absence of action by agents in the seconds after the shooting corroborated this story. So the case against Hickey rested on a supposition alongside reading a great deal into the inactivity of people seconds after a terrifying event. Certainly we can guess that the wronged individual in this theory would scarcely have gone to court if there had been any serious and material evidence that he had been involved in the death of Kennedy.

This particular episode is a warning about both the perils of stretching explanation and the likelihood this will happen around momentous events that are otherwise shrouded in mystery. Likewise, the suggestion that Kennedy had been killed by a conspiracy involving his Vice President Lyndon B. Johnson again has very little to commend it other than the fact that, with hindsight, Johnson appears to have benefited from Kennedy's death. Certainly we cannot use this as a satisfactory explanation since, whilst it might at first sight seem credible, only with substantial hindsight might Johnson be implicated and this indicates the need carefully to select the facts from which one is prepared to construct an explanation. The search for the beneficiaries of history, though tempting, does not fully explore the history either of human motivation or of the whole realm of causes – otherwise we would be condemned to comb history in search of a string of supposed assassins who just happened to have benefited from the deaths of others.

Now we come to consider, in a hierarchy of possible explanations, the ones that contain more credibility because they are based on the other facts that we cannot reasonably doubt. It has long been a favourite theory amongst many to suggest that Kennedy was the victim of a conspiracy emanating from Cuba. This theory argues that Kennedy was assassinated by a team who reported to Fidel Castro himself. Again this suggestion has a certain degree of credibility, because we know about the Cuban missile crisis and we also know that Kennedy fiercely opposed the regime Castro established in Cuba. We also know from subsequent disclosures that American intelligence, in the guise of the CIA, had undercover operatives in Cuba actively working to overthrow the revolution. They were also behind a number of plots against Castro himself and the Cuban leader had gone on record to denounce these plots and threaten reprisals. Again this looks like we can establish a collection of possible motives for the Cuban regime to seek the death of Kennedy. The plausibility of this explanation goes a shade further, however, because it is possible to link the most likely assassin, Lee Harvey Oswald, to Cuba. Oswald was known to be an admirer of the Cuban communist regime of Castro and actively made contact with the Cuban embassy in Mexico a matter of two months before Kennedy's assassination. However, it seems that what transpired after Oswald entered the Cuban embassy is not known and explanations that refer to this are based purely on supposition. Variations suggest Oswald was either paid money to undertake the assassination or agreed, on ideological grounds, to be the instrument of Kennedy's death. The apparent reasons these findings were not made public in the report from the Warren Commission are political ones, aimed at protecting the Lyndon B. Johnson presidency. Any anti-Cuban reaction against Castro would have given power to right-wing groups in America and would have damaged the political standing of the Democrats. Similarly the pressure to undertake military action against Castro's Cuba would have been difficult to resist when faced with evidence of their involvement in the assassination of Kennedy. We should note that whilst this explanation deals with some known facts about relations between Kennedy and Castro and the sympathies of Lee Harvey Oswald, this is, once again, where the irrefutable facts stop. Speculations using these suppositions are based on little more than guesswork and imaginative theories. Thus, whilst considerably more possible and likely than the 'zero game' theory, our ability to prove this slightly plausible sequence of events still eludes us because credibility, likelihood, and verifiability cannot be established.

For a long time another popular theory that has occupied the minds of commentators and speculators is the suggestion that Kennedy was assassinated by the Mafia and organized crime working in conjunction with the CIA. This theory supposes that in the years leading up to Kennedy's assassination the Mafia had worked closely with the CIA on its programme of destabilizing the Castro regime and had a record of significant involvement in the attempts on Castro's life. It is also alleged that the Mafia had engineered and illegally supported John F. Kennedy's election campaign through payments to ensure vote rigging. Supposedly in return the Mafia expected considerably enhanced status and power, combined with influence, running right the way up to the top. Kennedy was seen with some apparent friends of the mob, such as Frank Sinatra, and was rumoured to share a mistress with a leading mobster, Sam Giancana. When the apparent bargain was seen to be broken, the Mafia turned rapidly against the Kennedy family. Matters appear to be made even worse by the fact that John F. Kennedy's younger brother Robert had dramatically increased the number of state prosecutions brought against members of the mob. Again, clearly, we have a set of plausible, likely, and realistic motives that seem to hang together. Certainly many of the facts seem to be true. Robert Kennedy did target organized crime and John F. Kennedy did associate with personalities who had links to the mob. It is just as likely that the CIA could have formed a convenient working relationship with useful members of the Mafia.

However, all of this is some distance from placing a Mafia-sponsored individual in Dallas on that fateful day. However, this Mafia figure supposedly appeared when an individual called James Files came forward to confess that he had assassinated Kennedy. Although here we might have the testimony of a supposedly interested witness, we have very much to take on trust his testimony and believe it implicitly. Most historians faced with this dilemma would instinctively try and search for other corroborating evidence. Without this they would most likely still entertain considerable doubts about the truth of this particular explanation. So this explanation comes up short in our tests of credibility, likelihood, and verifiability – although in this case verifiability is the most pertinent issue.

In the aftermath of the death of John F. Kennedy it was a particularly popular theory to associate his death with a communist conspiracy emanating from the Eastern Bloc. Much of this theory relied on the testimony of Soviet dissidents and defectors who offered various accounts of elaborate plans to murder a number of world leaders, not just Kennedy. It was generally supposed that the KGB had engineered the assassination of Kennedy as some sort of reprisal for the back-down over the Cuban missile crisis of 1962 that had humiliated the Soviet leader Khrushchev. Again this theory does include some of the things we know to be true. There was significant American distrust of Soviet intentions in the years after 1945, and much of this permeated through to the American people, so it is scarcely surprising they were ready to believe in the reality of a Soviet plot. We also know that the CIA regularly debriefed defectors and dissidents and must have come across a vast range of stories and material. However, again, we are some distance from placing a KGB operative, or even KGB influence on Lee Harvey Oswald, in Dallas in November 1963. The KGB might equally have spread the story that it was responsible for Kennedy's death to enhance its prestige, both at home and abroad, and may have planted this information amongst dissident groups. Certainly it is tempting to conclude that this course of action was probably the most appealing one to the KGB. It waged their ideological war for them without the inherent dangers of outright confrontation if they were implicated in a messy assassination plot. This explanation is asking the historian to assess years of distrust and Cold War intelligence to imagine the actions of a hostile foreign power. As such it is following the same processes as the 'zero game'. This time the suppositions and collection of facts are considerably more credible because there are more of them and the plausibility of the explanation is based considerably more on real life experience.

The Warren Commission concluded that Lee Harvey Oswald acted alone to assassinate John F. Kennedy in Dallas on 22 November 1963. Certainly examination of the report, which appeared two years later, shows it to have been hastily assembled and to leave many questions unanswered. Many have looked at supposed inaccuracies, snippets of information, and pieces of unrelated material that seem to have been forgotten or overlooked. In the search for the truth of what happened this is exactly what a historian should be doing – assessing all information without necessarily jumping to conclusions, indulging bias, or being tempted to create anything resembling a conspiracy theory.

Lee Harvey Oswald supposedly shot at President Kennedy from the sixth floor of the Texas book depository. According to the Warren Commission, he acted alone and fired only three bullets. Thirty-five witnesses believed that they had heard shots coming from the opposite direction, the direction of the now infamously entitled 'grassy knoll'. This was, however, contradicted by the testimony of fifty-six witnesses who believed the shots had come from the direction of the book depository. But there was more material that corroborated the account of the thirty-five witnesses. One US secret service agent saw a large wound in the back of Kennedy's head which he presumed to be an exit wound, a story backed up by other evidence of other close eye witnesses. The doctor who attended Kennedy in the emergency room of the Dallas Hospital also believed that the damage visible in the back of Kennedy's head seemed clearly to be an exit wound. The bullet that supposedly killed Kennedy, according to the autopsy document, also entered the body of Governor John Connally. For this to have happened, the bullet would have had to have changed direction. The autopsy document also suggested the bullet that killed Kennedy entered his body at too low a trajectory to have been fired by Lee Harvey Oswald. This is the testimony of those closest to Kennedy in the moments when he died and consists of simple facts upon which no grand theory (conspiracy or otherwise) is built. In particular the testimony of the doctor examining the body must be taken seriously. This individual was an expert who had most likely seen similar damage in the past and was unlikely to have any bias or fabricated story to tell.

However, important evidence has also come to light in the shape of forensic examination regarding the sequence of events leading up to the firing of Oswald's rifle. This also alerts us to the fact that historians have to be quite creative in choosing the evidence they use and are always on the lookout for innovative evidence that can be used to answer the questions that history poses. This forensic examination was conducted in controlled conditions by US Marine snipers Craig Roberts and Carlos Hathcock. These two individuals reconstructed everything they knew about the Dallas assassination. They calculated the speed of vehicles, the direction and trajectory of shots, and evidence about the wounds sustained by all involved. They concluded that Lee Harvey Oswald could not have acted in the manner described by the Warren Commission account of the assassination. These qualified marksmen were unable to duplicate the expert gunnery of a supposedly comparative novice like Oswald. As historians we should take this as important evidence. First, it was compiled some distance from the event in both time and location and is thus not exposed to the hysteria surrounding it. It is material compiled by experts, so we can hope it is more reliable than some testimony that has been offered. But what is most important of all is that the methods used by Roberts and Hathcock are recorded and can be compared to similar experiments to demonstrate their potential accuracy. Besides this, all the measurements taken, the trajectories, different speeds, and assumptions about direction are capable of being reused by subsequent parties interested in the event. These statistics are even available for verification and for use by those who were (and are) sceptical about the conclusions drawn by Roberts and Hathcock.

So what, as historians, have we learnt from dipping a toe into the troubled waters of one of the most momentous events in American history? In looking at the world through the eyes of conspiracy theorists, we have initially learned the difference between a story and history. A story need only be a narrative that has a start, a middle, and a conclusion. It does not have rules about the pieces of material it uses, and it can weave these into a patchwork merely on a whim, or for the sake of maintaining interest or excitement. The story may only be capable of being believed if an individual enters into the spirit of the story. Thus conspiracy theories potentially tell us far more about the history of paranoia than about the history of the events they hope to explain. History is fundamentally different, since it tries to produce an objective factual account of events alongside an estimation of their causes and a conclusion about their lasting significance. First, we began the chapter with an attempt to make some sense of a quite bewildering array of different explanations. We looked at evidence and used our experience of the world to place these explanations in a hierarchy of the possible. We started by using the logic and experience we have gained from the world and the universe to dismiss the most strange and implausible explanations. We exercised our wisdom and what we knew of the world to conclude rapidly that mystical year numbers were realistically not responsible for the death of John F. Kennedy. We then went on to look at the slightly more plausible explanations, and noted how so many of these were based on supposition rather than anything that constituted fact. Last, we looked at fragments of information from eye witnesses and expert witnesses and noted that these were not ideologically driven to produce a grand theory about what had happened. Our endpoint was to look at the evidence we could probably consider to be most trustworthy. This gave us the most likely account of what happened to Kennedy in Dallas on 22 November 1963. We can be reasonably certain that Lee Harvey Oswald fired one or two shots at John F. Kennedy but we now have strong evidence that at least one other shot was fired and that this was probably the bullet that killed him. However, beyond this, as historians, we have to maintain a closer relationship with the facts and suggest that there is no explanation that completely satisfies us as to who pulled the trigger to fire this third bullet or why. And this is something that we should simply accept. The explanation is incomplete but asserting any further information as history without further evidence would reduce us to storytelling. At the moment, given the nature of the evidence, this is the explanation we should offer.

We have already looked at how historians establish credibility and judge the possible explanations of events and historical phenomena. Now it is time for us to look at the process of constructing these explanations for ourselves.

Looking at causes and causality

To evaluate causes and causality effectively, we need to think about methods of placing events in chronological order. Although simple, this particular task and its value should not be underestimated. Without a sound knowledge of a sequence of events and their correct order, all the most sophisticated theories in the universe are left floundering in the dust. Having assembled our chronological knowledge of what happened, we are now charged with putting this to its proper and valuable use. Very many explanations of what happened in history turn around the issue of causes and causality. There are a great number of debates throughout the historical world that look at the importance of causes. What caused the French Revolution and what caused the First World War are both leading questions which occupy historians of political and diplomatic history. What caused the Wall Street Crash and what led to the emancipation of women are questions that intrigue economic and social historians respectively. Historians interested in the history of the environment would similarly be keen to notice whether changes in the temperature and weather patterns over the centuries have caused human activity and society to alter.

Although causes are essential to our ability to offer historical explanations, we must be very careful how we assign causes their relative importance, ie we must ensure we are capable of assigning importance to both big and small causes. This is really telling us to be certain that we have looked at the whole picture to consider the immediate as well as the long term, in addition to underlying elements in finding causes for how and why things happen.

It is possible to be far too tunnel-visioned about this process, as historians look for the minute and small causes of historical events and phenomena. It was to counteract this tendency that the historian E.H. Carr wrote in the early part of the twentieth century (in his book *What is History?*) about what he termed the 'Cleopatra's nose' theory of history. This assigned the cause of great cataclysmic historical events down to the smallest unexpected and unforeseen cause. The theory, so Carr suggested, had a simple explanation for the Roman victory at the sea battle of Actium: Mark Anthony was so obsessed with the beauty of Cleopatra's nose that he failed to concentrate on the course of the battle and thus found his forces vanquished. Other old favourites blame the start of the religious Reformation of early modern Europe on Martin Luther's constipation, or in another version his continual and tormented sexual frustration as a celibate monk in late medieval Germany. Of course what was important in E.H. Carr's discussion of history was to suggest this was a laughingly narrow way of viewing the causes of past events. Historians endeavour to do more than merely look at one cause and build grander, more forceful, explanations upon this.

Thus our explanation of causality involves us looking very closely at one example of these particular 'big' and 'small' causes to see how they satisfy us as historians. Are we attracted to the power of the 'small' cause that seems to ignite sweeping historical change? Or are longer-running underlying 'big' causes more important? Yet, as most will already appreciate, it is the exact mix of small and big causes that determines what history we choose to write.

Haemophilia and the decline of the monarchy

In 1995 two biological scientists wrote a quite enthralling book entitled *Queen Victoria's Gene: Haemophilia and the Royal Family*.

D.M. Potts, a professor of population studies and family planning, and W.T.W. Potts, a professor of biology, wanted to study and tell the world about the impact of haemophilia on European history. They were especially convinced that nineteenth- and early twentieth-century history was overshadowed by the impact of the haemophilia gene on the royal houses of Europe. The condition of haemophilia is a systematic failure of human blood to coagulate and clot efficiently. It makes early life particularly hazardous for its unfortunate victims, since they risk bleeding to death as a result of even minor injury, rendering a normal upbringing almost impossible. With many modern medical advances the condition is, in the twenty-first century, not the obvious menace that it was – whilst it still makes life difficult for its unfortunate sufferers. It is a peculiarity of the syndrome that it only affects the male children born into a family. The female children remain unscathed, yet they still possess the gene responsible for this syndrome and are responsible for passing this onto their male children, with catastrophic results. Knowledge about this condition and its peculiarities was in short supply in the eighteenth and nineteenth centuries' and information was no more available to the highest in the land than it would have been to the most humble.

As many historians know, haemophilia afflicted many of the royal houses of Europe during the nineteenth century and the early twentieth. Perhaps the most famous sufferer was the heir to the Russian imperial throne, Tsarevich Alexander, who was executed by the Bolshevik government with the rest of his family at Ekaterinburg in 1919. Now, it would be something of an interesting historical piece of detection, and an exercise in tracing causality, to discover from where the unfortunate Tsarevich inherited the ailment. Who in his immediate family would have possessed the offending gene and from where had they inherited this? How much was known about the medical history of the individuals concerned and how could the tragedy that occurred have been prevented? This is the investigation of causality on a 'micro' scale so that, when we consider the status of the individuals involved, we have to ask some deeper 'macro' style questions. E.H. Carr's 'Cleopatra's nose' theory of history seemed ridiculous because it focused on a minute detail of the queen's appearance as a reason for the fall of an empire. The underlying point of this was to suggest the lives and decisions of great women and men have a deep resonance across historical events and the shape of the contemporary world these people live in or preside over. Thus our macro question about haemophilia moves from who spread it through the royal lines of Europe, to the effect this had on wider European history. The question becomes: did haemophilia destroy the old European monarchies by the end of the First World War? But this is also an invitation to consider the relative weighting of causes. In other words, it provides the historian with the opportunity to think about how the precise cause they are investigating *really did* contribute to the event or phenomenon they are examining. This is true of any historical explanation of events and processes – we have to find a hierarchy of causes and place them in an order of likely importance.

The suggestion that the health (or otherwise) of rulers has a profound effect on the nations and peoples they rule over has a long history. It was one of the central arguments of Edmund Gibbon's *The History of the Decline and Fall of the Roman Empire*, that the behaviour and decadence of Rome, led chiefly by its emperors, was a serious cause of its eventual collapse. Emperors from Tiberius to Nero and the infamous Caligula all demonstrated a variety of eccentricities and behavioural traits which crossed well over the border into insanity. Whilst some might seek to suggest these were important in Rome's decline, there are other historians who prefer to look elsewhere for underlying and more fundamental reasons. One current fashion blames Rome's decline on a disease pandemic (probably malaria) which left its defensive borders weakened and its commercial trading system almost paralysed. This again reminds us that causes must be weighted. The inattention of one or more emperors would be unlikely to bring down a tried and trusted administrative system and empire, generally considered capable of functioning on its own for some time. However, a malaria pandemic could very quickly and successfully paralyse this same system, rendering it fatally weakened against predators of various types.

Great men, great women, and causality

Whilst D.M. and W.T.W. Potts might try and convince us that haemophilia was the telling factor in nineteenth-century European history, we have to look at how it interacts with the other issues and historical developments of the period. In short, we would be naïve if we believed world-shattering events could hinge solely on the smallest of triggers. However, equally, it would almost certainly be a mistake to presume that these smaller causes do not have a part to play in the larger theories and trends that produce the broader sweep of history. Thus we need to find a method of putting these two together to see how both major and minor causes interact to produce such historical change. To do this we must first find a reliable method of assessing their relative value as explanations. So, let us see how this works to give a deeper understanding of the historical events associated with the turmoil of late eighteenth- and nineteenth-century political history.

We have heard something of the ideas of Messrs Potts and Potts, but we deserve to know more about the detail. We know for sure that Queen Victoria was a carrier of haemophilia and that she gave birth to three sons, yet only one of them, Prince Leopold, was a haemophiliac. However, two of Victoria's daughters, Princess Alice and Princess Beatrice, were carriers of the disease. Whilst medical knowledge was uncovering the truth behind haemophilia and its effects, it seems this was not known in royal circles. The essence of the argument by Potts and Potts is to suggest that the tendency toward haemophilia was inherited by the next two generations at an especially unfortunate time for monarchy. Interestingly, they see its effect not simply in its appearance, but also in its failure to appear at important moments – potentially turning this small cause arguably into a big cause. They speculate about what would have happened if the unfortunate Prince Leopold had lived beyond the age of thirty and also suggest history might have been altered if Leopold's son, Charles Edward, had inherited the haemophilia gene (even if, curiously, this was biologically impossible since it is passed down the female line). This last possibility leads the two authors to run away with themselves and their speculation, largely because Leopold's son had a key role in the rise of Hitler. In their attempts to play 'what if' games with history (what historians call counterfactual history), Messrs Potts and Potts actually speculate on the impossible in order to make their point about the supposed effects of haemophilia on European royal families and wider European politics.

Would history have been different if Victoria's eldest son, Edward Prince of Wales, had been the ugly duckling and Leopold had been a healthy child? Leopold became president of the Royal Society of Letters and vice president of the Society of Arts. The contrast with his elder brother the Prince of Wales, whose interests rarely extended beyond wine, women, gambling and song, was remarkable. Or what if Vicky (Victoria's eldest daughter) had been a carrier and perhaps her son, the future Kaiser, a haemophiliac, while Alice's family had been normal? There might not have been a World War in 1914 or a Russian Revolution in 1917. Or what if the unfortunate haemophiliac Leopold had fallen on his head and died five months earlier, or if Charles Edward had inherited

his father's lethal gene and died young? There might not
have been war in 1939 and 30,000,000 people might have
lived a lot longer.

Here Potts and Potts have decided on their own weighting of the
potential causes of war and revolution. Their weighting suggests
it is linked clearly and solely to the leadership and health of
'Great Men and Women'. This is a value judgement which has
shaped their interpretation of causes and their impact. For these
writers, it is personal leadership that is important in how history
is shaped. Other historians may equally be drawn to explanations
that encompass, for example, economic change. This is the
leading motivation behind Marxist explanations of history, which
see changes in the economic shape of society as the precursor
to other change. Beyond looking for, and potentially inflating
the importance of, small causes, there is a need to involve what
we know of larger causes. Our knowledge of nineteenth-century
history tells us that other factors worked to discredit monarchy
from the end of the eighteenth century onwards. This challenges
the weighting of the explanation offered by Potts and Potts. The
age of the absolute monarchs arguably came to an end with
the French Revolution in 1789, dealing a fatal blow to these
conceptions of kingship, and they would never seem the same
again. The world based on predestined aristocratic privilege was
challenged by new ideas associated with rights and democracy.
The French monarchy fell because it found itself in almost all
ways 'bankrupt'. It had financially exhausted itself in funding
wars against Britain, its chief imperial and economic rival. It had
lost the ability to rule through the dispersal and selling of land,
offices, and titles and could no longer marshal support from an
aristocratic system that was ineffective and exhausted. France was
also affected by a string of bad harvests, which left the monarchy
with the inability to deliver the reliable food supplies essential for
its survival. It should be noted that these are a series of 'big' causes

rolled into one. The 'Great Men and Women' perspective of Potts and Potts might be more attracted to the smaller immediate causes of Louis XVI's ineffectiveness and the hatred the populace harboured for his Queen Marie Antoinette.

Perhaps more important for the longer-term history of monarchy, and the societies over which it presided, was the fact that the French Revolution established a wider blueprint for how monarchies might be challenged and why. This links the idea of causes to historians' interest in specific processes and how they happen. Processes are important factors in examining change, since they show the transition from one type of state to another. How did the rural worker of eighteenth-century Europe become the factory worker of the nineteenth and twentieth? How did life expectancy improve over the course of seven centuries of Western history? The value of looking at processes is that our experience of observing one process can be used in our observation of another. In this instance what we know of the fall of previous monarchies might be valuable in deciding what happened to the French monarchy. Likewise what happened around the fall of the French monarchy might become valuable evidence of a process that might befall other monarchies. Indeed Karl Marx and other Marxist writers realized this and many books and treatises were written seeking to learn from the 'process' of what happened in 1789 and just after.

The French Revolution ushered in an era in which political and social changes would link with other critical changes to transform the world, making European societies unrecognizable from what they had been two generations earlier. During this century societies became more technologically and bureaucratically sophisticated and their governments became more skilled and familiar with the ways in which they could change society for their members. European societies had also developed empires and colonies which had stimulated consumption at home. The taste for apparently frivolous consumer goods meant such commodities fetched high prices and were consumed by a growing population with more disposable income. This new wealth created a bourgeois middle class, which simultaneously created further wealth and demand for the latest consumer products. These individuals became a force in the land in most European countries as the nineteenth century progressed, because they demanded some say in the government and taxation policies of these countries. This is another process at work, albeit a social one, and some historians likewise see the process of class formation as significantly important in the historical development of modern states.

The processes of industrialization and urbanization also created an industrial working class in many European countries during the nineteenth century. It could be suggested that the whole history of nineteenth-century politics was a contest between these two new social groupings, pitched against the remnants of the aristocracy and monarchy for political control of Western European societies. Certainly we can suggest that eruptions of political and social discontent quite regularly broke the surface during the nineteenth century, altering the prospects for the monarchies of a number of European countries.

But what of the suggestion of Potts and Potts that the haemophilia gene and its dangerous consequences may have been instrumental in the commencement of the First World War, the Russian Revolution, and the rise of Hitler? Once again we should look very closely at a hierarchy of large and small causes. If we take the first of these examples, the First World War, it is certainly possible to see other larger causes at work and importantly other histories playing themselves out. It is easy to focus on events in the Balkans in 1914, but the historian must look wider in the search for causes. First, it becomes important to see how European countries had entered a phase of intense competitiveness that suggested some sort of armed struggle on the horizon. By the second half of the nineteenth century most European countries were engaged in the process of building empires. Britain had secured parts of the Middle East, India, and important parts of south and central Africa. France, Belgium, and Spain had secured lesser but still significant territories. Germany, which had only unified quite recently, was very late entering this particular game, which became known as the 'Scramble for Africa'. It could be argued that Germany's failure to get involved in this process at the start meant that it was left with territories that were considered to be less desirable. However, the historian who looks even wider than this will get a broader perspective that taps into these other histories playing themselves out. Looking beyond the geography of Europe changes our picture of what the war may have been about. Italy, Portugal, and Japan also dreamed of such expansion and eventually had different reasons for entering the war, based on their own imperial territorial ambitions in Europe, Africa, and the Far East. So in this instance the historian should also be aware that an action may have its cause in some aspect of a longer-term history that is still ongoing.

It would have been one thing to have considered that Germany had missed out but, if you were a German politician, you might even conclude that Germany was potentially losing an undeclared war. Thus the search for some causes also involves engaging with the mindset of individuals in the historical past to understand their hopes and fears. In looking at some causes that shape the thinking of nations, it can be advantageous for a historian to consult an atlas. This rapidly conveys why Germany might have felt hemmed in by other nations in Europe. It has borders with a number of very powerful neighbours and could conceivably consider itself perpetually 'threatened' from both east and west. Similarly an atlas conveys why Japan might consider itself to be the premier power in South-East Asia, and it readily suggests where Japan might consider expanding its sphere of influence. Alongside this, knowing how the map looked at specific moments in the past also fine-tunes our knowledge of these geographical constants that might translate into causes and actions.

The newly unified Germany had engaged in an impressive modernization of its society, introducing conscription and quite sophisticated levels of technical education. This had been augmented by significant technological innovation in weapons manufacture, which led to what became known as an arms race. This was particularly noticeable in the area of sea power, where the advent of ironclad battleships pitched Western European navies against one another. This was a new area of warfare which engaged the whole population, not simply as combatants, but also as agents of public opinion that could both drive warfare onward and influence its outcome. This demonstrates the power of technological innovation and how this can persuade societies to envision their own power. This in itself has been seen as a cause of the conflict and the processes by which this happens. However, technological innovations also occur in areas such as the media, meaning that rulers now have to take account of public opinion or manage it. As we are aware, totalitarian regimes in the twentieth century have harnessed the power of this phenomenon with some success.

Similarly we might look more closely at the causes of the Russian Revolution to see how far haemophilia might have played a part in this. Certainly the heir to the Russian imperial throne, the young Tsarevich, was a chronic haemophiliac and would have been an especially sickly monarch. But to focus on this is to miss so many other things that were important. The Russian economy and society were still predominantly feudal at the end of the nineteenth century when all Western European states had, to a great extent, modernized. The Russian imperial crown had already seen a partial revolution in 1905 that had led to concessions that had brought about some tentative modernization, weakening the older feudal aspects of society. This awakens us to the idea that change is not a uniform occurrence, and a comparison with change elsewhere might create an idea of causality based on analysing the pace of change. Karl Marx thought Russia would literally be the last place where a revolution would occur because it did not fit his model of development. Marx was utterly convinced such a revolution would happen in the most developed of societies, namely the UK.

If we were still interested in the logic of 'Great Men and Women' ideas of causality offered by Potts and Potts, we would examine the behaviour of the Czarina Alexandra and her obsessive friendship with the charismatic figure Rasputin, which did as much to undermine the reputation of the Romanovs as the unfortunate accident of haemophilia. This is a reminder again about how change is not uniform and that this in itself (when observed by contemporaries observing events in their own time) can be a cause of change. Russian observers of the queen and Rasputin would have been irritated at how antiquated the twentieth-century Russian court, in thrall to charismatic superstition, would have looked in the eyes of the West. If an individual believes their society is suffering because it is backward, then this can be a powerful cause of change.

Thinking about the causes of change also means we should investigate the suggestion that Prince Leopold's son, Charles Edward, and his actions were so significant that his absence would have prevented the rise of Hitler and arguably the Second World War. Strangely the Charles Edward theory also removes power and influence from Hitler himself. This would be considered unsatisfactory to most historians who agree that Hitler's own dynamism was responsible for the position he was able to gain for himself and his ideas within the Germany of the post-First World War period.

Large causes are those that affect the grand scale. Almost by definition they are not isolated instances and most cannot be tied down to single events or happenings. They are also less tangible and obvious and, generally speaking, their impact is difficult to spot at any particular moment in time. Small causes are easier to spot and it is also easier to trace their impact. These can be single events or happenings or individual instances of something. Although these are not exclusive and obvious rules of thumb, most historians would agree that explanations tend to hinge around a combination of large and small causes. Whilst it is not universally true, it is probably likely that it is wise to distrust explanations that rely solely on either large or small causes. Each misses the explanatory power of the other. In assessing the importance of causes we draw on the balance of probability, and this uses our own knowledge of the world. As we discussed in relation to the Kennedy assassination, some facts about a historical occurrence seem obviously less important than others; by concentrating on the important ones we move more swiftly to a viable explanation. The other tools that help us with explanation, just as much as they do with assessing facts, are the yardsticks of credibility, likelihood, and verifiability.

Thus we have two fundamentally important items for our historian's toolbox. Investigating the Kennedy assassination has taught us about hierarchies of explanation and about testing the viability of these and the facts that are used to construct them. Both must pass our tests of credibility, likelihood, and verifiability. We have also learned about the importance of causes and causality, and how both greater and lesser causes interact in sometimes simple but also sometimes complex ways.

In this chapter we have looked at how history is constructed from facts, but it is important to note that one reason for wanting to know about our history is how it shapes our identity and that of others. This sometimes informs our desire truly to 'know' the past and the thoughts and actions of those within it. To achieve true understanding of this past, we must do our best to analyse how these people thought in the past about the world around them – in other words to understand their 'mentality'. One way of doing this is for the facts – or the history they create – to be retold to others. This creates a memory of past events and of past mentalities that so often shapes the present. Thus memory and its creation are important phenomena for the historian to understand. Now it is time to turn our attention to how history itself can be driven by the twin desires to 'know' the past through examining mentalities and to know about memory, and what this can contribute to our wider understanding of history.

4

Looking through the eyes of the past – history as mentality and memory

The quest to experience the past as others saw it

One of the particular attractions of history is the chance for individuals to encounter the past through the world of those who lived and experienced it – in other words to see and, as far as possible, experience what the pioneering social historian Peter Laslett described as 'the world we have lost'. In the wake of this quest to see the world of the past, one branch of history that has developed in leaps and bounds in the second half of the twentieth century has been the history of mentalities. For social historians it addressed an urge to know how people in the past thought about the world they lived in. Moreover they also believed that the approach to life of people in the past, and their own understanding of this world, governed the pre-occupations of that particular period and could shape how historians viewed it. This history of mentalities also looked at specific events, and the behaviour of people around these, to try and discern how the mindset of people in the past was different from our own. It was, for example, the pre-modern view of the human body, in which the various humours (bile, black bile, blood, and phlegm) became the means by which these societies explained the behaviour, actions, and temperament of people. An excess of one of these could explain mood or disposition (describing someone as 'phlegmatic', for example). This was obviously replaced eventually by explanations which began to focus on the mind, although initially only on the head. The nineteenth century witnessed a fashion for a pseudoscience known as phrenology (the study of the bumps on the head). This whole supposed realm of knowledge worked out a complex classification of each area of the head, indicating its role in influencing behaviour. Phrenologists were particularly interested in finding 'bumps' that could indicate benevolence, or the tendency to commit criminal acts. This approach to analysing behaviour eventually moved inside the head with the development of modern psychology and psychiatry. The last visible remnant of phrenology can generally be found in antique shops, which often stock porcelain heads with the different behavioural 'zones' marked on them.

This interest in mentalities that became popular with historians often really stemmed from three different directions which eventually merged into one. The first direction was the establishment of a branch of history that became known as the history of mentalities, and was very much a part of the revival of French historical and philosophical thinking that began in the 1930s. This created the history of what was termed in French *mentalité*, which also presumed that we could investigate the whole of history through tapping into the mindset of individuals in past societies. This was somewhat in contrast to the causality-driven approach mentioned in the second chapter. The second direction from which this interest in mentalities emerged was the growing interest in social history which was spawned by the late 1950s and early 1960s. This became a determined attempt to produce types of 'history from below', by which some historians wanted to overturn what they saw as elite-dominated history. Thus a history of the industrial revolution became less involved in recording the work of great inventors and innovators and instead concerned itself with the thoughts of those at the sharp end of industrial change who tried to resist its unpleasant consequences in a number of ways. Similarly, the oral histories of those who served in wars, or worked through the establishment of state-funded forms of medicine, provide a contrast to a history that would record the actions of the politicians who were the architects of this. From these came numerous attempts to recover the history of the forgotten and those who had been 'hidden' from history. Thus labour, black, women's, gender, and post-colonial history all arose to provide a thoroughly different perspective on a very male, Euro-centric, and white historical tradition. The third, and final, inspiration for the history of mentalities came from a growing, sometimes grassroots movement that sought empathy with the past. This last idea was inspired by everything from the boom in heritage and museums through to the lure of historical novels, plays, and television series which themselves entered a golden age from the 1960s onwards. Eventually this trend culminated in a desire to empathize with the near and remote historical past. The word 'empathy' became so fashionable that it found its way on to secondary school curricula and was something of a buzz word for a time.

In some respects, this desire to recreate the lifestyle and behaviour of individuals in the past has also encouraged the growth of what many historians have called cultural history. That is, the desire to produce a history of our shared practices, beliefs, and assumptions and how these influenced past societies. Understanding and getting close to the mentality of people in the past is to gain an important insight into their culture – in effect the practices of life that mattered to them and why they mattered. This exploration might also be used to see how these past mentalities might have set patterns for our own practices, or instead if they were radically different from them. Only with knowledge of Japanese military codes, and the beliefs they created amongst adherents, does it become possible to understand why thousands of Japanese kamikaze pilots were prepared to commit suicide in the course of attacks on Allied shipping during the Second World War.

Despite going in and out of fashion, the quest to empathize with the sometimes remote historical past is vital because it teaches one of the most important skills about understanding the past – that is, the ability to bridge the distance in time between oneself and an individual in the past. In most instances their world looks strange when we try and approach it, so we can only fully understand it by looking at the mental world these people inhabited and placing ourselves firmly in their shoes. To do this and truly to understand their world we have (perhaps strangely) to *unlearn* history rather than learn more about it. That last statement may sound odd, but our path to understanding the past can be obscured by our knowledge and grasp of what happened since the historical period with which we are trying to empathize. Sometimes we need to forget what happened after this period to understand fully the implications for actual people in past situations. I once asked a class of students why the female inmates of a Victorian prison were far more likely to get ill during the summer. After several minutes thinking, they were at a total loss to explain this curiosity and offered everything from asthma to pregnancy as possible answers. The prevalence of stomach and related bowel complaints, which were endemic in Victorian England, were a result of water-borne bacteria that multiplied in warm weather and infected water supplies that were never purified before consumption. This would not occur to a group of second-millennium students who had been brought up with several generations of plentiful and efficient plumbing and sanitation. This was something which had itself been taken for granted by their parents and probably their grandparents well before the millennium generation had even been thought of! The fact that Victorian women were also so often second-class citizens in the quest for a decent diet (since they frequently had to forgo food so that male breadwinners could gain essential nourishment) was also lost on this group. To understand this, the students I was teaching had to forget years of better health, food, welfare, and grasp the past's gendered attitudes to nourishment.

To consider this issue differently, the early nineteenth-century desire to pray for deliverance from the cholera epidemics which swept through the Europe in the 1830s and 1840s seems odd or primitive to us. But if we forget the subsequent scientific discoveries about waterborne diseases and the cholera bacillus, the sanitary reforms enacted by numerous government-appointed reformers, and later drives to improve public health, the reaction of these individuals who called on God to save them becomes more explicable. In the absence of knowledge about rational causes for the disease, it was a lot easier to consider that different European countries were being punished for their descent into sin. This was a world which believed in the clear possibility of divine intervention, and a God who had visited plagues upon Egypt was quite capable of doing so upon contemporary Europe.

Thus, understanding the mentality of people in the past is an important way to understand a vast number of things about past societies. We get to know how people within a specific period think, we learn about the norms, the concerns, and the mindset of the period, and we learn about how individuals in that period thought the world functioned. Once we understand this we start to know much more about the processes of this past society and the choices people made that influenced subsequent history. In short, we obtain an accessible window on the past that may make us reflect on our own mentalities and how these may have evolved from this past. Thus a history of events is not necessarily *just* one of causality.

To demonstrate how we can do this we are going to look at the thoughts of two societies in the distant past. The first of these examples tells us about a humble miller from a remote area of north-eastern Italy who found himself forced to tell the world about how he thought it operated. The second is a more general investigation of what past attitudes to death and the culture surrounding it can tell us about different societies and different historical moments. This second example also tells us about the ways in which the legacies of these societies (the historical sources) can be used to piece together both moments in time and changes over time.

Domenico Scandella: peasant philosopher

In 1976 the writer Carlo Ginzburg published an enthralling and astonishing book entitled *The Cheese and the Worms*. This was an exploration of the mindset of a sixteenth-century miller called Domenico Scandella (alias Menocchio), from an area called Friuli in the north-eastern corner of Italy. Ginzburg had come across this individual whilst researching the history of witchcraft in a series of papal inquisition papers. Menocchio had been a particularly outspoken man who had extremely definite opinions about religion, belief, and the authorities he encountered in his rural existence. These opinions he had tried to spread amongst the populace of his locality and it was this that got him into trouble with the Inquisition. But when this organization took him in for questioning, they could scarcely have prepared themselves for what they were going to discover.

Generally speaking, those arrested by the Inquisition did their best not to give anything away. Menocchio was something of an exception since he readily admitted he had spoken the words the Inquisition found religiously unorthodox, and worryingly he also stated that he was prepared to tell others about what he believed. Menocchio's initial disclosures were quite standard denunciations of the clergy, the authority of the Pope, denial of the Eucharist, and the value of Masses said for the dead. These ideas would have been recognized by the Inquisition as part and parcel of the dangerous heresies of the late medieval period. But Ginzburg had noted that Menocchio's views, taken as a whole, did not fit in with the conventional heresies of the age. What set Menocchio and his opinions firmly apart was his statement, which conveyed to all who would listen how he viewed the creation and operation of the universe – and it was unusual to say the very least.

Menocchio believed that the universe was born out of rotting matter, and all the different elements that were an original part of this were mixed together and changed into vibrant living things. He then had to use a simile to explain precisely what he meant by this and chose to suggest it was the same as cheese being made from milk. He then went on to say that this 'cheese' became home to 'worms', worms which crawled around inside the cheese, and that he believed these to be 'angels'. This was a particularly odd way for anyone to describe the creation of the universe and Carlo Ginzburg became intent on tracking down what had contributed to the construction of Menocchio's strange and idiosyncratic view of the world.

Ginzburg did not have to look very far. Fortunately the Inquisition recorded which books had been confiscated from Menocchio. These included the Bible and the Qur'an as well as a biblical commentary, a work by a Dominican friar, Boccaccio's unexpurgated edition of the *Decameron*, and the *Historia del giudicio* (an anonymous poem), alongside other Italian works such as the *Fioretto della Bibbia* and a traveller's chronicle by Sir John Mandeville.

Ginzburg initially thought that he would find all the answers to his questions about Menocchio's mindset through intensive reading of these particular works. Although other works which could not be identified had been mentioned, Ginzburg was confident the answer lay in Menocchio's own personal library. However, the issue was not as simple as this since it gradually became obvious that the ideas, considered as a whole, were a noisy collision of different things, which meant something else was clearly at work.

The answer lay in accepting that Menocchio was not taking inspiration from these works wholesale but rather reading selectively, latching on to passing ideas and phrases that appealed to him from his reading or his conversations with others. Ginzburg described this realization in these terms:

> When we compare, one by one, passages from the books mentioned by Menocchio with the conclusions that he drew from them (if not with the manner in which he reported them to the judges), we invariably find gaps and discrepancies of serious proportions. Any attempt to consider these books as 'sources' in the mechanical sense of the term collapses before the aggressive originality of Menocchio's reading. More than the text, then, what is important is the key to his reading, the screen that he unconsciously placed between himself and the printed page: a filter that emphasised certain words while obscuring others, that stretched the meaning of the word, taking it out of its context, that acted on Menocchio's memory and distorted the very words of the text. And this screen, this key to his reading, continually leads us back to a culture that is very different from the one expressed on the printed page – one based on an oral tradition.

It was certainly true that some of his ideas could be traced back to his reading. For example, Menocchio had denied that Christ was the son of God because he had noted that the *Fioretto della Bibbia* had described St Joseph as Christ's natural father. Similarly Menocchio had read in Sir John Mandeville's work that the crucifixion of Christ must not have happened, since it contradicted the idea of a righteous and just God. He also drew from this work, and a famous 'medieval legend of three rings', important lessons about religious tolerance. He suggested that everyone thought they had been brought up in the correct religious law, whether they were Christian or Muslim or heretic. Menocchio even, astonishingly, tried to convince the Inquisitor of the positive virtues of religious tolerance. Ginzburg noticed here that Menocchio was arguing from a blend of his learning (however quirky and selective that might be) and his memory of folk and fairy tales.

This was ultimately to be the clue to unpacking how this sixteenth-century miller had constructed a worldview that would astonish the Inquisition, and the history scholar who found him some four hundred years later. This man had created his mental world which he presented to the Inquisitors, from the books he had read and from his memory of popular stories and tales that he had heard in the area where he grew up simply by following his trade. But what of his assertion that the world and its creation was like turning milk into cheese? And from where on earth had the suggestion emerged that worms, which were really angels, crawled in this cheese? The answer that Ginzburg discovered is intriguing; the particular area of north-eastern Italy where Menocchio originated from was notable for producing a certain type of cheese which is still produced today.

This cheese was (and still is) fashioned in a ball shape and laid in dark damp caves to mature for some months. When it is extracted and prepared for consumption it is normally sliced in half and, more often than not, the middle is discovered to be rotten and crawling with maggots! This was the comparison he had reached for in trying to explain the universe. Menocchio now stands as a man whose mental world was constructed by a collision of his book learning, his knowledge of folklore, his thinking about the scriptures and about the world in general, and his experiences of sixteenth-century peasant customs and practices. All this had happened in defiance of authority and by the accident of Menocchio's own psychological makeup. The universe he constructed made more sense to him than the universe constructed by the Catholic Church or the individual philosophers he read and thought about. It was a part of his own individuality that he sought to combine all these elements and change them into something else – just as cheese and rotting matter were transformed into the universe he inhabited. Beyond this there is a huge wealth of further information that might be used, and it is certainly possible that further interrogation of the minutiae of material in the Inquisition's records and elsewhere can continue to yield information and insight.

But to return to one of the themes of the chapter – the lasting value of the history of mentalities speaking to us about a particular society – what else have we learned from the story of Menocchio? Watching him interact with his questioners, we start to learn much about why the Inquisition and the Catholic Church wanted to control and save people from their unorthodox belief systems. We also learn an astonishing amount about reading habits in rural sixteenth-century Italy. We now know which books were in circulation, how they were circulated, and who read them. We also know much more about the process of reading, thinking, and assimilating that took place amongst those who read these books. It is also now possible to know that people do not simply pick their ideas up from their reading. There is a collision between these ideas and the lived experience of the individual as they try to make sense of the world in which they find themselves. It is the historian's job to make sense of this confusion and to recapture the past these people constructed for themselves as their own sense of their own present.

The hour of our death: dying, mourning, and cultures of the past

Many historians interested in the history of mentalities have focused on the fundamentally important human experiences that are common to all of us and thus have a long-term history. It is precisely this long-term perspective that allows many to use these experiences to investigate the mentality of people in the past and how they thought about these common human experiences in some very different historical contexts. In the second chapter we discovered how a history of love and affection could be written and we noted how some experiences really were quite universal. Our example here is the history of death, which is able to show us a somewhat different story since it emphasizes the differences between our society and past societies, and how they thought about the end of life. In many respects it is these differences (rather than the actual historical events we explored in the last chapter) that comprise the essence of history for some historians.

These common human experiences were a particular source of fascination for French historians in the first half of the twentieth century who formed themselves into a group they called the Annales School. This term literally meant 'story', with the implication that they saw their task as providing a broad and sweeping 'total' history of human experience – one that explored these differences over time. One individual who drew inspiration from this idea was a French historian called Philippe Ariès. He had originally approached the history of childhood and concluded that it was a comparatively modern invention, which only latterly saw children treated with compassion and consideration by adults. Thereafter he approached the long-term history of death aiming to tell a wide-ranging story that would let us into the mind and mentality of past societies. He looked at a range of sources to investigate how people died in medieval society. These included poems, stories, and medieval romances. We have already encountered literary sources in the second chapter but it is worth reiterating that literature does not necessarily simply reflect society. It also offers an ideal world that could frequently influence the thoughts of individuals.

THE ANNALES SCHOOL

The Annales School was effectively created by the work of two French historians, Marc Bloch and Lucien Febvre, who were active in the first third of the twentieth century. Both had grown dissatisfied with the narrow nature of political history and instead wanted to rejuvenate the study of the subject by adopting an approach which borrowed insights from other social science disciplines such as economics, psychology, anthropology, geography, and sociology. For them this gradually involved leaving behind the prevailing history of their time with its interest in personalities and dates. This was replaced in the Annales School approach by a sort of overarching history which wanted to see society as a whole. Thus this approach demonstrates a wide range of interests in artefacts, structures, buildings, and institutions – evident in the work of a third member of the Annales School, Fernand Braudel. A lingering interest in groups in society and the great undercurrents of history that played themselves out over very long time spans was likewise a legacy from ties to social science and anthropology in particular. Thus they were similarly interested in fundamental changes in things like marriage, community, childhood, and death. The Annales was also the place where interest in the history of mentalities really flourished, since this offered lasting proof of how great underlying changes had altered the human condition.

Ariès noted how many male deaths were actively portrayed as romantic and simply heroic since, as warlike knights, their often short lives were lived within an aggressive and martial culture. Whilst this image was a literary portrayal of death, which would not have been widespread throughout European cultures, Ariès also looked at other evidence that these societies left behind. He decided that this society wanted to accommodate death to the requirements of life by sharing its impact in the community at large. When he looked at tombs that littered the medieval churches of Europe he was able to make some tentative conclusions, and we can ourselves follow in his footsteps to investigate these ideas. Many of the tombs of men in the high medieval period he examined echoed the military and martial aspects of their lives.

Those who had been on crusade were depicted in full armour and chain mail and often with weapons and a shield, which seemed to suggest that military identity was important to the men of such a society and that death in battle was a very real possibility. Later in the Middle Ages monuments began to exhibit more gruesome decoration, with skulls or occasionally depictions of the corpse being devoured by worms. These seem contemporary with the arrival of plague and the 'Black Death' throughout Europe, the message being that the human body was transient and corruptible – a truth made self-evident when plague ravaged most of Christendom. This was also evidence of a worldview that placed a greater emphasis on sin and its consequences from the fourteenth century onwards.

The link between plague and a society that believed such occurrences were a divine judgement from God naturally follows from this evidence. For example, the sudden emergence of plague in fourteenth-century Europe influenced how medieval men and women thought about life and death. This appears to change the way they think about these phenomena and historians noted both a growing sense of guilt and preoccupation with macabre funeral monuments resulting from this. For fifteenth-century people plague was a visitation from God and an invitation to meditate on his judgement on men and women and their inevitably swift demise. By putting these images on the graves of their loved ones, medieval men and women sought regularly to remind themselves of the constant presence of potentially immanent death. This becomes still more understandable when we remember that life expectancy was much shorter than it is now, and this reminds us that death is thus not as powerful a presence in our own lives as we routinely live into our eighties and nineties. However, the very late medieval period also produced tombs and monuments which had started to move away from the apparent obsession with warfare. In some parts of Europe it had begun to be fashionable, and wholly acceptable, for individuals to celebrate their status as prosperous and successful merchants. This was a new existence far removed from the warlike men of a previous generation. Expenditure on death and its accompaniments (everything from expensive tombs to financial legacies to feed the poor or to say holy Masses for the souls of the departed) became a method of establishing and commemorating the achievement of high status. This in some respects could be seen as undermining the idea of the sudden and heroic death of the individual in battle, arguing strongly that it belonged to a previous age.

Moving forward in time to the early modern period the evidence offered by tombs and monuments starts to change. Increasingly it became fashionable to present husband and wife together, very often at prayer. It also became common for depictions of the family's children to appear on these tombs. This was significant because it started to redefine identity within society and what society saw as an ideal. This change meant that society had moved away from the medieval depiction of the heroic individual to the idea of the family tomb. Whilst this said important things about the family and its development as a more modern alternative to war, or the Church, it also indicated to historians that individuals hoped and perhaps expected their own family to continue into eternity. But in some respects these monuments were also a demonstration of worldly success, in which a lavish and imposing tomb would readily demonstrate to the rest of the population that this particular family had been successful and had arrived in society; a message that would reflect well on surviving members.

However, historians also have to consider the religious beliefs of the period and how these may have influenced attitudes to death. Religion is central to how individuals make sense of the universe and how they construct and envisage their place within it. Many European countries were Catholic and believed in the religious doctrine of purgatory. This stated that individuals were not, by any stretch of the imagination, guaranteed a place in heaven; they would instead be placed in purgatory – a sort of holding area between heaven and hell. Thereafter it was the task of the living to say prayers for the repose of the soul of individuals unfortunate enough to be in purgatory. The idea was that such prayers, said regularly enough and in sufficient numbers, would allow them into heaven. The footprint of this religious doctrine could be seen in many places throughout Europe, where rich and prosperous individuals had left money in their wills to employ priests to say Mass every day for the repose of their soul (in effect asking for the individual to be admitted to heaven). Sometimes these individuals even constructed purpose-built chapels and left significant sums of money to support the priests who served there.

One of the chief grievances of those who wanted to reform the Catholic Church was the selling of indulgences – effectively documents issued by the papacy which gave individuals partial exemption or 'time off' the period they would have been serving in purgatory. Whilst this doctrine was central to the Catholic faith, Philippe Ariès noted how in many respects it meant that the dead were in a much more intimate and close relationship with the living than we are used to in modern times – they were in a sense still with us. Prayers for the dead, essential if you believed you were helping them to escape purgatory, meant that the dead were much more readily in the thoughts of the living on an everyday basis. Ariès also looked at the evidence which seemed to suggest that the dead were in closer *physical* proximity to the living. The parish churchyards of medieval Europe were much closer to the population than the subsequent municipal graveyards, and the later phenomenon of cremation with its destruction of the body, placed them. These parish graveyards, so Ariès noted, were places where the local community often took their leisure or sometimes conducted trade or held their local market. In this respect the living were co-existing with the dead.

The coming of the Reformation and the religious changes it brought eventually put an end to the idea of purgatory in the countries and the areas of Europe that became Protestant. This change was signalled, according to the English historian A.G. Dickens, by the gradual dwindling of legacies left to employ priests and to build chapels for the saying of prayers for the repose of individuals' souls. Examining evidence from a large number of wills and last testaments written before, during, and after the important period of the Reformation, Dickens concluded that the practice of leaving such legacies had already begun to fall into disuse in the period before sweeping religious changes occurred. Perhaps this was indicating the permeation of a significant change in attitudes towards death amongst the wider population. Slowly, legacies from wills began to demonstrate that Masses no longer needed to be said for the departed and instead the money was directed to provide charitable help for the living. However, we should be wary of seeing this, or any other, change in mentality as happening instantaneously or overnight. Since Dickens wrote on the Reformation, other historians have uncovered evidence of older beliefs surviving for much longer than anticipated – certainly some time after the change had been actively encouraged by official policy.

Moving on from this era Ariès noted how the idea of death changed in the romantic period from the mid-eighteenth century and how there came to be a developing idea of the 'good' or 'ideal' death. We should note that this ideal 'good death' was very different to the martial and sudden deaths of the medieval knight. This model 'good death' was actively contemplated and generally speaking drawn out, so that the individual could be surrounded by their family and comforted to the end. The reconciliation with God, and the slow and peaceful nature of such deaths, were also in this instance intended to comfort the living and there is much evidence to suggest that they did precisely this. This model was so effective that nineteenth-century atheists actually created their own parallel, in which a peaceful death was preceded by a conscious witnessed denial of Christianity.

When he came to consider the modern world and its approach to death, Ariès emerged from his study manifestly dissatisfied with how the twentieth century (and arguably the period beyond) dealt with death. As he expressed admiration for the family-orientated 'good death' of the nineteenth century, he noted how the modern world had increasingly sought to thrust the dead away from the living. The places of burial were out of town, away from the centres of population now, and performed no other social function for the living than as a repository of human remains. The increasing importance of cremation was effectively removing the dead completely from the consciousness of the living, making death an increasingly rare occurrence within human life, destined to be marginalized from the modern consciousness. The more Ariès looked at it, the more he saw that contemporary death also appeared to be considerably less satisfactory. Instead of dying in familiar surroundings amidst family members, the modern individual was likely to find their death dominated by the medical profession with its specific procedures and demands – the individual in the modern world would die alone surrounded by the machines of medical science, an 'invisible' death. This analysis led Ariès to conclude that the past, at least in this instance, was a better place. This served as an important reminder that if history could reclaim and articulate knowledge of the past, then the modern world should be capable of judging the value of these practices and, if desired, stage a discreet return to them. In this light we might consider such a return to have been in the minds of those who created the numerous hospice movements of the last quarter of the twentieth century. But, interestingly, even here we encounter a clash of mentalities, since many atheists are suspicious of such institutions because they step away from clinical, scientific, and ultimately rational approaches to death. The definition and meaning of this universal experience thus remains a battleground.

But, as I hope we have discovered, this brief insight into the history of mentalities has shown us that exploring the mental world of others is a particularly useful and valuable method of uncovering the secrets of past societies themselves. In this, learning how to empathize with the past is an especially effective way of understanding it. However, this is also accomplished by using history to remember the past, since a society's attempts to commemorate and remember also signal to us what was important for that society. We also do this ourselves by transmitting our own important memories and perceptions to subsequent generations. As we shall see in the next section, these memories have a potent impact on subsequent societies.

War, memory, and constructed history

Arguably there has been no more overwhelmingly important experience in the twentieth century than that of war. One of the ways that we know this is because the landscape and architectural fabric, of Western countries in particular, actively reflects this. Very few towns or cities do not have some memorial to the dead or fallen of both World Wars – spectacular catastrophes that left scars of loss and suffering across many continents.

Whilst Ancient Greece used words to commemorate King Leonidas and his three hundred Spartan warriors who defended their homeland from the Persians, the last two centuries have tended to combine words with physical commemoration in stone. For our purposes, as historians, both of these are texts and memorials which teach us the significance of what individuals thought about these events. Sometimes it is possible to see directly how these memorials convey important stories about the events they commemorate. Significantly, they also tell us about how events in the past are brought before audiences and how such audiences interpret them. They also suggest how such stories of the past are transmitted and changed over time. In short, history often exists as a species of memory which is capable of being used to construct stories that have a long life and, importantly, have power. As a result historians have to be aware that such memories have a potent existence that shapes the present as much as the past. These memories can be vital to the personal identity of individuals, of groups, and indeed of nations. Whilst it is obviously important for historians to tell the stories behind such memories, and to seek the truth behind the events they commemorate, there is also a wider and deeper purpose behind a historian's interest in memory. When we see these war memorials, and monuments and the stories they speak of, it becomes possible to read and construct the meaning of memory. In this process, history becomes the record of human stories that transcend the events they commemorate – not simply a window onto the past, but also a picture of how the past has been constructed, reconstructed, and contested. These are message boards that deliberately transmit information and sentiment directly from a past age to our own. This means historians must collect and catalogue these messages, and decipher what they all mean.

The American Civil War: rebellion or a war between the states?

The American Civil War is probably the first war to be commemorated and remembered as a collection of conflicting memories. These variations are perfectly demonstrated by the different titles that the period has garnered throughout America. Many people now know it by the name of 'The Civil War' which most history books use. This is also how the world outside America has been persuaded to see it. However, it has been given other names which convey different interpretations, bias, and prejudice alongside other contrary and uncomfortable memories. Some in the previously Confederate south know the war by the term 'the War between the States', suggesting a deeper unnecessary quarrel about rights and jurisdiction that overwhelms the other arguments someone from the northern states would have grown up with. In some southern states there is a still more strident phrase used – 'the war of northern aggression'. This informative and unequivocal explanation swiftly exonerates the southern states from any culpability in the causes of and resulting suffering caused by the conflict. In addition to the names given to the war in history books, it is still possible to hear authentic voices from the time, and learn how some of the views they expressed have survived into modern times if we listen (or in this case look) closely enough.

Monuments to the war and the fallen exist in small towns throughout the north-east, the south, and the mid-west of the (now) United States. Each of these bears inscriptions and testimony to what the local inhabitants thought the 1861–5 war was about, and why it was fought. In northern states the conflict is described as one in which the combatants were fighting defensively to protect a united nation and the northern view of America as a union betrayed. The monument at Portsmouth (Ohio) described it as 'The war for the preservation of the Union', whilst the monument at Warren (Ohio) saw the war as having been 'fought to preserve the Union of the States'. But there are stronger voices to be found that describe the war as caused by the dissent and supposedly 'treacherous' action of the Confederacy. The Greenfield (Massachusetts) monument described the war as commemorating soldiers who were involved in 'suppressing the Great rebellion and for the preservation of the National Union'. The monument at Kenosha (Wisconsin) remembers those who 'victoriously defended the Union on land and sea during the war of the Great Rebellion 1861–65', and the monument at Barry (Illinois) commemorates 'the Union soldiers – War of the rebellion 1861–65'. Although fiercely defensive of the Union and the northern outlook of 1861, these views still persist. In some northern states individuals wish the Confederacy had won the Civil War. Their reasoning behind this is that the independent north and south could have thereafter developed separate societies in the manner they both wished. These people thus view the American 'United States' they inherited as a dubious compromise, arguably pleasing no one. Again this perspective has its own southern counterpart in the state of Texas' annual symbolic application to leave the Union.

Attitudes in the previously Confederate south display a dogged separatism and a dislike of the war's victors. Monuments in the previously Confederate states tell a different and equally fascinating story. Commemorating a war in which individuals, nations, and groups have been defeated is a painful and difficult task. It involves trying to remember courage in the face of overwhelming odds and trying to forget the painful story of capitulation. It also strives to remember sacrifice, whilst maintaining the justice and lasting value of that sacrifice. Yet also those left to remember have a duty not to inflame the sensibilities of the victors. Many southern monuments chose to use politically neutral phrases such as 'to our Confederate dead' or 'those who wore the grey'. The role of southern women in the war and the taste of defeat are remembered at the city of Texarkana (Texas) with the inscription:

> O great Confederate mothers we would paint your names on monuments that men may read them as the years go by and tribute pay to you who bore and nurtured hero-sons and gave them solace on that darkest day, when they came home, with broken swords and guns!

But this also reminds us how much history and memory is sometimes written by the victorious, overshadowing the very different views of the defeated. History is the propaganda of the victors who get to choose the version of events told to subsequent generations. Intriguingly this phenomenon was realized by the Confederate General Patrick Cleburne (known as 'the Stonewall of the West') who was killed at the battle of Franklin on 30 November 1864 and whose words are quoted on the memorial at Altamont (Tennessee):

> Surrender means that the history of this heroic struggle will be written by the enemy. That our youth will be trained by northern school teachers, learn from northern school books their version of the war and taught to regard our gallant dead as traitors and our maimed veterans as fit objects of derision.

Other memorials, however, tell us much more about the southern viewpoint and begin to show the war as a more complex phenomenon. The monument at Taylorsville (North Carolina) noted that many fought for the Confederacy 'not for the preservation of slavery but our greatest heritage, states' rights'. This dramatically places the blame for the war on the side of the Union, whose actions were considered to be unconstitutional and an assault on freedom. Other monuments also pick up on this theme. At Blakely (Georgia) the inscription commemorates those who 'cheerfully offered their lives in defence of the right of local self-government'. In White Springs (Florida) the conflict is called 'the war for southern independence' whilst the monument at Greenville (Mississippi) was 'For those who encountered the perils of war in defence of the sacred cause of rights and constitutional government'. Some wrapped constitutional rights into a protection of the southern homeland. The monument at Columbus (Georgia) celebrated 'Confederate soldiers who died to repel unconstitutional invasion to protect the right reserved to the people and to perpetuate forever the sovereignty of the states'. Some linked their battle with the War of Independence to give themselves further legitimacy. In St Louis (Missouri) the Confederates who fell 'fought to uphold the right declared by the pen of Jefferson ... Battled to preserve the independence of the states which was won from Great Britain'. Perhaps most partisan of all is the memorial at (ironically) Union City (Tennessee) which remembers the 'Confederate soldier who ... has preserved the Anglo-Saxon civilization in the South'.

This independence and resolutely southern attitude is still maintained as a folk memory which pervades popular culture from folk and rock songs (such as The Band's famous *The Night They Drove Old Dixie Down*) to television programmes and films like *The Undefeated*, *The Outlaw Josey Wales*, and *Gone with the Wind*. This is an example of how memory can be passed down to subsequent generations. Battles even continued in the world of rock music in the 1970s where Neil Young's critical, northern-inflected song *Southern Man* was stridently answered by Lynyrd Skynyrd's anthem to the south entitled *Sweet Home Alabama*. For some people in the south the Civil War has, arguably, merely slid beneath the surface and manifests itself today in rampant distrust of the federal government, which can make its presence felt at state, county, city, town, and individual levels. Thus in this sense historical memory generally fuels and empowers the persistence of such feelings into the contemporary world.

Nonetheless it is also possible to detect other, later voices, which spoke up in valiant attempts to heal the wounds of the 1861–5 war. At Greensboro (North Carolina) there is the 'No North – No South Monument' which used instances from the War of Independence to show that America was a united nation before the 1861–5 war. Noting that Nathanael Greene was a northerner campaigning in the south, whilst George Washington was a southerner campaigning in the north, the monument stated they were both patriots who fought for American freedom. Thus memories can be actively used to stimulate and promote reconciliation.

The Second Boer War and Afrikaner loss

Some memories are also rewritten and deliberately reconstructed to make political points in the modern world. Sometimes the very timing of these rewritten memories reflects the success of related memories elsewhere and these can copy precedents from other places. This is particularly true of monuments commemorating those who perished, which very often borrow aspects of the past as well as other ideas from the present. The first twentieth-century war to seek deliberate and visible commemoration was the Second Boer War (1899–1902). In British towns such as Leicester and Worcester the service and sacrifice of the common soldiery of the local regiment receive monumental commemoration in statues and monuments. The soldiers from these and other cities are also remembered far from home on the cemeteries of the African veldt. But the Second Boer War is also remembered for the introduction of concentration camps. These were originally designed to 'concentrate' the civilian Afrikaner population in military-run camps behind barbed wire. The idea was to deny the Boer irregular troops the emotional and logistical support of their families whilst they were fighting a guerrilla-style war away 'on komando'. This term was later to be synonymous, notably in the Second World War, with irregular ways of fighting and forms of warfare.

Unfortunately, the British lines of supply were grotesquely inadequate and the camps simply could not cope with the influx of civilian captives. As a result thousands died of starvation and disease. This caused a profound scandal in South Africa and amongst radical circles back in Britain. In South Africa the memory of this outrage is commemorated at the sites of these camps. One of these locations, a place called Irene, just outside the modern city of Pretoria, is a good example of how this dreadful incident has been remembered and politicized. If tourists visit this camp today an unexpected sight is likely to greet them. Originally, the women and children who died at Irene were commemorated with individual memorial plaques, often placed by surviving members of the victim's family. Understandably these memorials tell a tragic and poignant story of loss and the memory of such loss. Each individual was remembered by their family in a variety of ways special to each. The plaques were, for much of the twentieth century, the centre piece of the memorial park and cemetery. However, today's visitors will discover that these personal memorials have been removed from their central position and placed on the side wall of the park. In their place stands a vast and monolithic monument on which the names of the victims are inscribed. On this monument each name appears identically alongside its neighbour. This has the unmistakable effect of turning hundreds and thousands of episodes of individual loss into one vast incident of sustained collective loss.

Many other memorials to the Second Boer War in South Africa also display this approach to making the country's defeat an occasion for the commemoration of collective suffering. For the historian this is intriguing and prompts other questions, not simply about how this war is remembered, but how the stories told about it are capable of being altered to make obvious political statements. The first thing we notice here is the characteristic of the Afrikaner 'nation' collectively to commemorate its own history, both for its own consumption and for the eyes of the outside world. This is because the Afrikaners believe themselves to have been given a solemn mission to colonize and bring civilization to Africa – in some versions they went as far as to equate themselves with the Israelites to become the chosen race. This is plainly evident from looking at the country's foremost memorial – the Voortrekker monument. This remembers the so-called 'Great Trek' which involved hundreds of Afrikaner families setting out from the southernmost part of South Africa, the Cape area. These 'Voortrekkers' headed north in search of land to farm and settle. The 'Great Trek' became a search for a homeland, which clearly in their minds and mentalities imitated the biblical search of the Israelites. Until subsequent history created a 'day of reconciliation', the sixteenth of December each year had been called the 'Day of the Vow' or 'Day of the Covenant', in which Voortrekkers had been victorious over a force of Zulus after they had prayed earnestly for God's help. Certainly historians have emphasized that the Afrikaners came to see themselves in this way, casting themselves as the newest version of God's chosen people.

This important and formative memory comes back to us when we consider the state of the memorial park and cemetery at Irene. This concentration camp site, and others like it, received their makeover in the years immediately following the Second World War. Thus by marginalizing the individual losses in favour of collective commemoration the South African government of the immediate post-Second World War period was making remembrance a political act, deliberately borrowing from the Jewish memorializing of the Holocaust. Effectively this reminded visitors of the earlier creation of concentration camps and who their earlier inmates and victims were. As such this equated their suffering with that of the Jews in the Holocaust – the persecution of another chosen race. These memorials also reminded Afrikaner visitors that they were a chosen race, at a time when South African identity (or specifically Afrikaner identity) was in the process of redefinition that would culminate in the implementation of apartheid. In this atmosphere it is scarcely surprising that Afrikaners would promote their identification with the concept of the chosen race.

Since the eclipse of white minority rule in South Africa the political meaning of these memorials has taken on a new series of meanings. New stories are being written over the conventional histories of the war. At a conference to commemorate the centenary in 1998 a discussion arose about how many African tribes had been exploited and treated as expendable cannon fodder by both the Afrikaners and the British. A black African speaker rose from the audience to speak eloquently against this view. He argued that, far from being exploited and naive, many African tribes made calculated judgements about which side to support, based on how each of them could benefit. Thus in the era of black majority rule it was time to remember the black contribution to the war in a way that was not condescending and guilty about the actions of both white Afrikaner settlers and the colonial powers. To witness this was to observe the memorializing of the South African War adapted to the needs of the multiracial and integrating rainbow nation in the new millennium.

Other conflicts of the twentieth century have also been remembered in a number of different ways and each of these tells us much about the act and function of memorializing. They also make clear to us that the task of the historian is to notice, analyse, and record these changes, because knowledge of how and why memories are constructed enables us to treat them rationally and critically.

Ireland and its wars of the twentieth century

The southern Irish memory of the First World War is riddled with conflicting messages and meanings. It is possible to argue that the outbreak of the First World War saved the island of Ireland from a dangerous confrontation. The northern Protestant loyalists had defied the implementation of Irish Home Rule and become an armed camp. Nationalists in the south had equally been campaigning for its installation. The war enabled the British government to suspend the proposal, thereby, for the time being, calming hostilities in Ireland. When the First World War broke out, thousands of Ulster Protestants and Catholics from the remaining twenty-six counties volunteered for military service. Considerable numbers died from both communities, yet how they were remembered by both could not have been more different. The previous example of the South African war was about remembering and restating, and how the ongoing nature of these processes problematized both the past and the present. The example given here, related to Irish history, is much more about the consequences of forgetting and how eventually resurrecting memory can be used as tools of reconciliation.

Ulster's contribution to the First World War was, and is, a cherished popular and official memory. This is scarcely surprising since it represented the ultimate sacrifice in the cause of loyalism. Commemoration of this became so essential that it developed into a symbol of the loyalist cause in all sorts of contexts. Even graffiti that appeared on the sides of houses during the Troubles of the 1970s and 1980s remembered this. The exploits of the Ulster division on the Western Front were directly identified with the struggle of Irish Protestant paramilitaries. Indeed the IRA Enniskillen bombing of November 1987 (in which eleven people were killed and sixty-three injured) was considered an especial outrage because it targeted a Remembrance Day parade and struck at the very heart of loyalist identity.

In what had now become the Irish Republic the soldiers, sailors, airmen and women who had served the British Empire in the 'war to end all wars' were largely forgotten. They were frequently portrayed as mercenaries rather than loyal subjects fighting in a noble cause. Indeed as late as 2010 surviving relatives were still trying to locate and place monuments on the graves of these servicemen who had been buried on the Irish mainland in unmarked graves. Not only was their sacrifice ignored (actively hidden even) but its significance had been dramatically blotted out by other political events on the Irish mainland. At Easter 1916 Irish nationalism spectacularly broke the surface in an armed rising in Dublin that briefly established a provisional government of an independent Irish republic. This was put down by the British army, but within a few years the 'Easter Rising' was a central and living memory for Irish nationalism. The memories of the leaders who had been executed (Patrick Pearse, James Connolly, Tom Clarke, and others) assumed they had been martyred in a noble cause. In this particular instance the tributes and sorrow that might have been lavished on veterans of the First World War were instead reserved for the martyrs of the 1916 Easter Rising. Although memorials to the First World War were built in what became the Irish Republic they were, within a comparatively short time, neglected by the populace, in stark contrast to their treatment in Northern Ireland and on the British mainland. Indeed the fallen of Ulster were commemorated by one of the very first monuments, erected at Thiepval in northern France.

The memories and their polarization were of course a function of the delicate political relations between the triangle of London, Dublin, and Belfast. The change to this state of affairs was also inevitably brought about by events in Ireland's political history. The 'Good Friday Agreement' of April 1998 and the 'Peace Process' fundamentally changed the politics of the island. It was especially interesting to note how the barbed and partisan views of the First World War became harnessed by the British and Irish governments as a medium for a statement of reconciliation. For the historian it was especially important to note how memory does not exist in a vacuum and is regularly called on to speak to a new generation with an altered or adjusted story. Likewise it proved how history is equally a tool for stoking conflict, or alternatively for bringing about reconciliation.

On 11 November (Armistice Day) 1998 in Belgium, the Queen of England, the Irish President Mary McAleese, and the Belgian king opened a memorial park and monument which brought together both sides in Ireland's sectarian conflict. The 'Island of Ireland Peace Park and Tower' seized upon a fortunate coincidence to unite both sides around mutual sacrifice. In 1917, at Messines Ridge on the Western Front the 36th Ulster Division went into battle alongside the 16th Irish Division. Both Divisions sustained roughly the same number of casualties (averaging around 30,000 troops each). Today this sacrifice and service is remembered in this park and by the tower at the centre of it. Spinning out from the tower like a giant fan are four plots of Irish yew trees to commemorate the fallen of all four provinces of Ireland. Along one side of the fan are a series of commemorative stones which record the casualties sustained by both divisions in the fighting around Messines Ridge. Next to these stones are fifteen others which contain the names of all the Irish regiments involved. Bisecting the fan is a long pathway which leads to a viewing platform from which the central tower can be seen. The trajectory of this path is exactly designed so that the sun at 11 AM on Armistice Day (11 November) is in exact alignment with the tower, perhaps echoing the words spoken at the annual festival of remembrance: 'at the going down of the sun and in the morning we will remember them'. The viewing platform itself is in the shape of an Irish ringfort that would have been indigenous to all thirty-two counties of Ireland and it faces an impressive stone tower, again of pre-medieval, Dark Age design. The tower itself was built with stone reclaimed from a demolished almshouse in Mullingar. This in itself was an example of history literally being recycled into a new form. Although it might at first appear to be a happy ending of sorts, this instance provides us with a reminder that history is rarely neat and tidy. In the years after its optimistic inauguration the maintenance of the park became something of an issue with wrangles about who was responsible for funding its upkeep. In its way, this perhaps echoed arguments of long ago about whether those who fought for England were pressed into doing so (suggesting British responsibility), or were free volunteers who had made their own choice to fight in a heroic cause.

Anzacs at war

On the other side of the world in Australia the memory of the First World War took a profoundly different and unequivocal direction. Although Australians served with heroism and distinction on the Western Front, and won many medals in the campaign in Russia after the armistice, it was a decision by the then First Lord of the Admiralty, Winston Churchill, that changed the war utterly for the Australian nation. In 1915 he championed an attack on the Turkish homeland through a landing in the Dardanelles at the heart of the Ottoman (Turkish) Empire. This was a strategically important strait along the Allied supply route to Russia. The impetus against the Central Powers of Germany, Austria-Hungary, and the Turkish Ottoman Empire had slithered to a disappointing halt in the mud of the Western Front. Thus Churchill's gamble was approved of as a means of supplying a blow that would knock an already weakened Turkey out of the war. Troops were to land at Suvla Bay and push the Turkish forces back, triggering surrender. The expeditionary force contained British and French, alongside Australians and New Zealanders, who were grouped together in what was known as the Australian and New Zealand Army Corps. The troops belonging to this grouping rapidly became known as 'Anzacs' – a name that was to reverberate through history. When the troops landed they met stiff resistance and lessons that should have been learned on the Western Front seem to have been forgotten. The terrain was mountainous and offered superb cover for the Turkish riflemen and machine gunners. The realization that well-prepared troops in defensive positions were very difficult to defeat had not dawned on the Allied commanders, despite the experiences of the Western Front. Likewise they failed to realize the necessity of bringing to bear superior resources to defeat an enemy and, in the result, the expeditionary force at Gallipoli was woefully underprepared and undersupplied. The war had also reached a stalemate simply because the average rifle in the hands of the infantryman of each combatant power was capable of inflicting death and injury from almost a mile away with astounding accuracy, reliability, and speed. At what became known as 'Anzac Cove' the Turkish soldiers were able to fire on the troops below them, making movement impossible and resulting in the Allied troops digging trenches and ramparts, in disappointingly direct imitation of the situation on the Western Front.

Whereas the war in Europe was characterized by mud and rain, the war in the Gallipoli campaign, as it came to be known, was fought amidst searing heat, flies, and sub-tropical disease which laid low many of the soldiers. Like the Western Front, this theatre of war eventually settled into a sad stalemate which simply consumed men and resources at an unacceptable rate. Eventually it was decided to make a tactical withdrawal and end what had become a military embarrassment. Although not technically a defeat, the episode was quite far from a military success. Yet it is remembered with intense fondness and pride in Australia. Indeed it is seen as a fundamentally important moment in the creation of Australian nationhood. Every town and city in Australia has memorials to the fallen, whether they died on the Western Front, in Mesopotamia, or in the Gallipoli campaign. However, Australian war memorials, unlike elsewhere, display the names of those who died and also of those who returned. This was because the Australians who went to war between 1914 and 1918 were solely volunteers who served willingly for the British Empire. Such an attitude was important since when it was suggested that conscription be introduced, many who opposed it were supporters of the war and active servicemen. They argued that 'allowing' conscripts into the Australian war effort would undermine and taint the service of the brave volunteers.

Australians also focused on their part in the Dardanelles campaign since their contribution to it had manifestly displayed the Australian spirit. It was a tough campaign in tough terrain and the soldiers were tested to the limit. The stalemate brought about improvisation which showed off what became legendary Australian resourcefulness to the full – an image which tapped into the country's pioneering culture. Moreover, there was also a lingering distrust of the British generals who in some narratives (such as the film *Gallipoli*) appeared to be reckless with the lives of the troops under their command. At the National War Memorial in Canberra there is an impressive memorial to those who fell at Anzac Cove and throughout the Dardanelles campaign. Yet outside the building is a statue which brings the heroism down to a more human scale. It displays an individual leading a donkey on which is resting a wounded soldier. The memorial commemorates the service of John Simpson Kirkpatrick who became famous for his exploits as 'the man with the donkey'. Simpson has all the credentials of an Australian war hero. He joined up immediately upon the outbreak of the war in August 1914 and then displayed personal valour and resourcefulness in commandeering a donkey that had been used to carry water supplies, instead turning it to the service of the wounded. Simpson repeatedly led the donkey through dangerous terrain, braving sniper fire, to collect and save wounded men and bring them back to Anzac Cove for medical treatment. Invariably his luck ran out and he was killed, once again saving wounded men, on 19 May 1915. This image simultaneously remembers independence, courage, resourcefulness, pity, and compassion – all traits that almost any national identity would wish to claim gratefully and gladly for its own. Yet this whole campaign and the history told about it also tells us something else about the power of myth. The casual observer could be forgiven for thinking that there were *only* Australian troops involved in the Gallipoli campaign. This is because the Australian desire to remember easily overwrites the desire of British and French governments and armed services actively to forget what, for them, was not even a terribly heroic failure.

ANZAC Day is a national holiday in Australia and is marked by commemorative marches throughout Australia. Whilst interest in it waned for a little while, it has recently been making a noted comeback, especially with young people. But the footprints of this memory also lie in some unexpected places. Each time the Australian cricket team leaves Australia to compete in an Ashes series against England, it avoids a non-stop flight to England or one that has the conventional Asian stop-off points. It chooses to make a stopover in Turkey with the explicit intention of visiting the battlefield at Anzac Cove. The tour management insist that the tour party are photographed in the trenches wearing the famous bush hats that characterized the visual image of the ANZAC warrior. This interestingly equates the national sport with notions of duty, courage, and Australian nationhood. The cricketers who have the chance to wear the famed and coveted baggy green cap are seen and portrayed as following in the footsteps of their ancestors – the ANZAC heroes of Gallipoli. Belatedly realizing the importance of this act, the England cricket team (in 2009) commenced the practice of visiting its country's own sites of sacrifice during the 'war to end all wars' – the trenches and cemeteries in Flanders.

But even here the historian has to be wary to spot and include the attitudes of those who doubt and evade the orthodox view of even something so uniformly celebrated as ANZAC Day. During its early stages there were those who were perplexed and disappointed by the capacity for the day to turn into drunken revelry. Similarly, quite strident voices were prepared to criticize ANZAC Day as an oversimplified glorification of war and all its terrors. In some ways modern Australia defined itself in opposition to the memorializing of the past. Perhaps the best representative of this was the folk singer Eric Bogle who wrote about an old soldier retelling and remembering his experiences from Gallipoli. Amongst many other counter-cultural anthems,

Bogle did what he could to distil the futility of the Dardanelles campaign and its real impact on living men.

> So they collected the cripples, the wounded and maimed
> And they shipped us back home to Australia
> The legless, the armless, the blind and insane
> Those proud wounded heroes of Suvla
> And as our ship pulled into Circular Quay
> I looked at the place where me legs used to be
> And thanked Christ there was nobody waiting for me
> To grieve and to mourn and to pity
>
> And the band played 'Waltzing Matilda'
> As they carried us down the gangway
> But nobody cheered, they just stood and stared
> And they turned all their faces away
>
> And now every April I sit on my porch
> And I watch the parade pass before me
> I see my old comrades, how proudly they march
> Reliving the dreams of past glory
> I see the old men, all twisted and torn
> The forgotten heroes of a forgotten war
> And the young people ask me, what are they marching for?
> And I ask myself the same question
> (*And the band played 'Waltzing Matilda'*)

Reactions in Australia to the Gallipoli campaign's centenary have likewise not necessarily been so readily prepared to buy into the story of Australian nationhood and resourcefulness. Australian network television's lavishly filmed *Gallipoli* was significantly unpopular in many circles, as audiences felt more ambivalent about this episode of the nation's story. The series was accused of being jingoistic and encouraging Australian identity to be warlike and unquestioning in providing over-enthusiastic troops for ill-judged foreign interventions on behalf of other world powers. The history of this event came to be judged against the lessons and misgivings promoted by subsequent historical events such as military intervention in Iraq and Afghanistan.

This is an especially potent reminder that the twentieth century has borne witness to the fact that not every part of the culture that has gone to war is prepared to remember that war with pride. Whilst the Second World War produced memorials in concrete and words to match the eloquence of those for the First World War, there were also memorials that spoke still deeper of loss and the political impact of some battles. The memorial at Kohima, the battle at which the Japanese onslaught at the gates of India was turned back, says 'Go and tell of us and say, for your tomorrow we gave our today'. Such an explication would not have sounded out of place commemorating Leonidas and the Spartans, or those at Masada, Leningrad, or Kut, honouring the sacrifice of warriors throughout the ages. The power of each of these lies in the poignancy and brevity with which they reflect not only political impact, but also the sacrifice that people were happy to make, so that the society, politics, culture, and the very essence of their nationhood could remain intact.

But the twentieth century has also seen the use of memory and the memorial to evoke loss as much as the nobility of sacrifice. Each May in Russia sees a celebration of the end of the Second World War in Europe. For many years it was also traditional for a bride and groom on their wedding day to leave wreaths and flowers on the monuments that commemorated the war dead. This deep vein of remembrance should not be surprising when we remember that, out of the total number of those who died as a result of the Second World War, one in four of these was a Russian man or woman. However, in West London Russian actions are remembered quite differently. Near the centre of the Polish émigré community exiled by the partition of Poland in 1939–40, they remember their loss in a political manner. In 1943 the Germans discovered a mass grave in Katyn Wood near Smolensk, deep inside Russia – an event portrayed in the recent Robert Harris book and British film *Enigma*. Poland had been invaded in 1939 by Germany in the first days of what became the Second World War. Within a short period of time an agreement between Moscow and Berlin had partitioned Poland. The mass grave contained the remains of four-and-a-half thousand Polish soldiers and shockingly, for the time, the body of a female Polish serving soldier. Obviously it was a controversy as to who had been responsible for the slaughter – had it been Hitler's SS or Stalin's NKVD who had assassinated these soldiers for no obvious or apparent reason? The Germans had found the corpses but, despite their poor record of behaviour in Eastern Europe, it was a mystery as to why they should bring this atrocity to the world's attention if they were going to be thought responsible.

What was important for the purposes of our chapter is that the Poles who produced the eventual memorial to the atrocity at Katyn Wood defiantly dated the deaths of their comrades to 1940. This unequivocally stated that the Russian NKVD was responsible for the atrocity, in defiance of British and American support for the Russian version of events which blamed the Germans. It was also using history to emphasize a historical dimension to their current exile. Yet to make sense of this émigré community's judgement we have to understand one hundred years of Polish history, in which the country had been squabbled over by both East and West. A desire for liberation from the yoke of being a central victim of Europe's great predators motivated the Polish community in West London. By defiantly proclaiming the entry date of their exile to be 1940 they had also tried to discredit the ideological power of the communist bloc. For historians, what this said was that an independent Poland and Polish identity would be commemorated as having died this day. With the post-war influence of Russian Communism spreading like a mantle across Eastern Europe, the Poles in exile linked the atrocity of 1940 with their nation's current oppression. In 2010 it was finally admitted in Russian documents that Stalin's NKVD was responsible for the atrocity. The story, sadly, has a tragic end, because the aircraft carrying the Polish cabinet to a memorial service crashed near Smolensk, killing a number of leading members of the government. Thus, lamentably, the massacre of Katyn Wood wrote yet another unfortunate chapter in Poland's memory of suffering.

America and Australia have also found ways to express their respective memories of the Vietnam War which spanned the 1960s into the mid-1970s. While evangelicals and old soldiers gather around memorials to the dead of Vietnam, the memorializing is mixed and confused. In Australia, in contrast to the country's pride in the sacrifice of two World Wars, the victims of Vietnam are not remembered by name. In the USA the Vietnam War was a problem because it had no secure definition of victory, leading to its meaning being lost and confused. Only belatedly did the USA construct one central memorial where individuals remember loss, friendship, and family, but very little else. Yet the memorial to the Vietnam War is primarily in celluloid. Films like *Go Tell the Spartans*, *Coming Home*, *Born on the Fourth of July*, *Full Metal Jacket*, and *The Deer Hunter* do the remembering for American society. Ultimately these may colour the final memory of the war fought to defend the West from Communism. Perhaps the absence of the memorials that their European forebears had built in stone and concrete meant that it took a new generation to examine what had happened that had so traumatized American society. Because monuments had not produced an established way of remembering the Vietnam War, it persuaded a subsequent generation to do this through stories which it took to the cinema.

When can we stop remembering the events of war and suffering which we seek to commemorate? It might seem a legitimate question for a historian to ask, but our lesson from most of the examples above is that cultures do not always allow individuals to stop remembering and that it is very frequently an act of identity to remember. Yet sometimes, through the act of reconciling the past with the present, we have been able to allow some actions to be forgotten.

An equally valuable investigation would be to look at how our commemoration and memory changes over time. Why is the memory of conflict changed by the historical context in which the particular war concerned is remembered? Each contemporary society rewrites and sometimes tries to write over the memory of past commemoration, with varying degrees of success. When those Irish servicemen from the First World War are disinterred from their unmarked graves and buried with proper headstones and memorials, this will be a reconciliation. However, it will also potentially destroy the memory that they were once buried in unmarked graves. This is both reconciliation and society deciding it is time to forget.

Wars bring history to the centre of people's consciousness and we have seen how this memory changes, even in the comparatively small space of 150 years. Moreover we have learned one of the tasks of a historian is to ask how memory functions in particular ways. But importantly, in our attempt to make sense of these, we are also persuaded to ask why such memories are shaped to tell particular stories. It is this latter question which brings us, as historians, the most fruitful and vital answers.

5

The secret and profound history of ordinary things

Many people become interested in history as a result of an encounter with its power and meaning within their daily lives. Often individuals are drawn to investigate their own background and to trace their own family tree. Ancestors, the histories of our forebears and their lives, and what these say to subsequent generations, are fascinating. They provide, for many people, an instant connection with the past that is at once familiar and exotic. The past may be, to many, 'another country', but through tracing our family tree it is peopled with our own relatives and thus with individuals with whom we can empathize. Alternatively some people are drawn to historic buildings or landmarks within their own locality which are of some antiquity, and this frequently ignites an interest for them in the past of their own neighbourhood and community. Likewise many grasp history through the simplest of items that surround us in our daily lives. Even the humblest aspect of our lives has a past and sometimes a rich and detailed history. This can make us appreciate how life and experience have changed and make us look at the supposedly mundane and the ordinary with a renewed interest. This has persuaded historians to write books about the influence of (amongst other things) 'Salt', 'The Potato, 'Cod', 'Fish and Chips', and the importance of five different crops for the history of civilization.

Very often this interest in the otherwise mundane can also help us engage with the idea of historical identity, which we noticed was extremely important in the last chapter. The fate of civilizations, communities, and nations has been shaped by some individual items, objects, and foodstuffs. The list of apparently mundane items provides ample evidence of this. The potato has had a profound effect on the history of the Irish nation, both for better and for worse. Likewise cod has had a far-reaching influence on the seagoing cultures of Scandinavia and the eastern seaboard of the Americas. Other aspects of our lives are also influenced by such things. The five crops which shaped civilization included the opium poppy, which produced opiates to enable medical treatment under anaesthetic, but also the unpleasant prospect of addiction to some of its products. Likewise cotton enabled cheaper and healthier clothing to be produced, which raised visible living standards alongside its enormous impact on the economy of slavery and underdevelopment in the southern USA and the Indian subcontinent. In this instance one crop made possible raised living standards and vast wealth in one sector of the world, whilst impoverishing and arguably retarding the development of another sector. Thus it is possible to see changes within mundane things reflecting wider changes within society. They thus become a prism through which to see the preoccupations and agendas of past societies and perhaps to examine how and why these underwent changes in response to social, economic, and political circumstances. This examination of what is around us can make us think about the twin concepts of continuity and change.

Within this search for links with the everyday experience of our ancestors in the past, we can discover that societies develop traditions which often shape and perhaps even govern many aspects of our lives. Such traditions appear to be an influence on contemporary practice and are often seen as a precise and tangible link with the past. Reactions to such traditions can vary, however. They can be celebrated and even promoted as essential to the preservation of identity in a changing world, or they can be considered outmoded, nonsensical, or even barbaric by those who object to the message that the tradition celebrates. Historical enquiry can begin anywhere and it teaches historians to think how ideas, commodities, and physical objects can play a part in the historical process. It also forcefully tells us that the appearance and function of these objects is not random and that their creation or consumption fits into a wider pattern that tells us about aspects of human history. The fact of their survival and decisions about their importance also make these remnants a part of our heritage. This is an important concept which is interlinked with the concept of identity. Identity is constructed from the pieces of historical identification that heritage gives us. Many countries in Europe preserve a range of aspects of their past because they are representative of the component parts of identity. This is the collective story of a nation, community, or group of people. Thus modern Germany preserves evidence of its land being occupied by the Romans. But it also has evidence of the early modern period when it existed as a number of city states and principalities with their own separate history. This can be contrasted with its unification during the nineteenth century, which eventually spawned monuments to its victory in the Franco-Prussian War of 1870. Some relics of the twentieth century also describe and portray defeat in two World Wars and (for a time) separation into two nations. Yet Germany also has a heritage of mundane items such as food and drink and these, being both different and similar to those elsewhere, portray both a unique and similar experience to that of other nations.

This search for tradition and investigation of the everyday can extend to considering the production of things, their consumption, and their place in the contemporary culture and how this differs from the past. This chapter takes the reader through an investigated example which shows the grandeur of history that can be contained within aspects of simple everyday life. It is a history of things, rather than a history of people which dominated the subjects investigated in chapters 2 to 4. This chapter considers beer both as an inheritance of the past and also as a medium that carries real messages (or traditions) from the past. Likewise, facts about beer's own past and present can inform wider histories of subjects such as work, leisure, consumption, class, place, travel, migration, and colonialism. However, beer is also invested with what we might call essential 'values' from the past and occasionally with a history that is not always what it seems when we scrutinize it closely.

Beer has been brewed and consumed since time immemorial. It was probably discovered as a result of primitive man mistakenly leaving wheat or barley to sit in a container of water, producing a sweet draught which had a pleasantly mild effect on his mood and temper. Brewing is first recorded in history amongst the ancient Sumerians, Babylonians, and Egyptians, appearing in frescos on the walls of tombs and, in the case of the Babylonians, in the epic story of Gilgamesh. This in itself gives the drink a considerable tradition and heritage from the ancient world, before subsequent layers of history also make their contribution.

In the medieval period brewing became one of the main industrial occupations of the Church's monasteries. Because of their powerful social and economic position these could purchase or obtain barley and other grain from their farmlands in both regular and sufficient quantities to supply the locality or town in which they were situated. Through trial and error the monks of medieval Europe developed considerable expertise in the formulation and production of beers. This, as we shall see, left a substantial legacy for subsequent societies and drinkers. The link was further reinforced by the fact that a number of medieval clerical figures and saints were linked to beer-related miracles. Although St Nicholas is thought of as Father Christmas, he was also the patron saint of brewers and coopers (barrel makers) in medieval Germany. This reminds us that the transformation of water, malt, and yeast into beer was still regarded as connected with divine blessing – indeed some brewers used the name 'God is good' for the magic ingredient of yeast. The medieval hermit Hildegard of Bingen (1098–1179) also wrote a scientific treatise on the natural world which discussed the virtues of using hops in beer. This simultaneously shows us that the medieval world's scientific investigation generally occurred behind monastery or convent walls, and also that much scientific investigation at this time revolved around perfecting foodstuffs and drink, a vital pursuit in this society. Beer was important because it provided viable nourishing alternatives to bacteria-ridden water supplies that could readily kill people!

It was only in the nineteenth century that such methods changed as major brewers were able to put steam and malleable metals (products of the industrial revolution) to good use. Breweries became factories in all but name, as the ambitious scale of beer brewing and selling enterprises grew significantly. Beers began to be nationally, and occasionally internationally, recognized as both technical and cultural obstacles to its distribution disappeared. This was the forerunner of a modern, fully multinational industry which generates multi-million-pound and -dollar revenues for companies that now not only run and own licensed premises, but also have stakes in other industries as well as those related to the leisure sector. Breweries sponsor arts festivals, literary prizes, and sporting events and are now fully integrated into Western culture in a way that reaches far beyond their function as a manufacturer and retailer of beer.

Exploring history through drink

When you decide to have a beer, wherever you are, you are embarking on a journey into history and the heritage of civilization's relationship with alcohol. This also demonstrates another of our tools of analysis, essential to the work of an historian – the ability to see the important historical connections between ideas and objects. By focusing on one object this can start us on a path to considering a wider history with more sophisticated analysis and explanation. In other words we move beyond simply cataloguing the things bequeathed to us from the past and start to place them in patterns that explain the past. This process is easier to do if we start with familiar objects. We may know the recent past of these and through our familiarity we may even have contributed to their recent history ourselves. Thus we are instantly aware of some aspect of their history as well as potentially regarding them as familiar. This same familiarity may help us engage with the past and understand an object's significance. This also enables us to compare such familiar objects and our reactions to them with objects that are strange and initially beyond comprehension. This allows the opportunity of comparison in historical development to offer complementary analyses and histories of such objects.

Depending on which country you lived in, your journey to a beer would be somewhat different. If you lived in America your decision to go for a beer would probably involve thinking about how to get to your destination. In America your local bar would probably be some distance away from your residential area. Alternatively this distance may have persuaded you to stay at home to have a beer. If you had your beer at home in a can you may have decided to take it fishing with you, to take it to a sporting event, or even to drive somewhere else to drink it. This perhaps reflects an aspect of American culture less understood in other parts of the northern hemisphere – the interest in the great outdoors. Some of this was quite culturally ingrained and protection for this behaviour would sometimes appear in local and state laws – sometimes in contradiction to more recognizably modern safety considerations. For example, it was only in the early 1990s that the state of Texas outlawed drinking *whilst* driving!

If you lived in the UK then you would be more likely to walk to your destination to have a beer. This is not to say that there is no history or heritage associated with driving and beer in Britain. Many of the country's main trunk roads are littered with large multi-bar public houses. If closely examined many of these betray their own past. Some might have been eighteenth-century coaching inns that provided warmth and hospitality between the major towns and cities of the day. Some might have appeared as late as the 1930s in a recreation of the coaching inn tradition – but this time to serve the needs of the motor car which had suddenly become both desirable and affordable for an increasingly important portion of the population. This coincided with lower-middle-class incomes expanding, and these pubs served a clear purpose and met a growing demand from those for whom mobility and the car were symbols of status. Many of these public houses have oak panelling, cross gables, and thick glass windows in a style which was described as 'Tudorbethan'. This indicated that it had borrowed architectural ideas from both the Tudor and Elizabethan periods to create the illusion of antiquity. This made customers feel more comfortable, as well as giving them the impression that they were following in a tradition and in the footsteps of their ancestors. Thus the public house was here functioning as a site and vehicle of instant heritage, providing an immediate contact with the history of things.

If you were attempting to have a beer in the UK, your search for a public house would also take you into further exploration of beer and its history. The actual location of the 'pub' often betrays important aspects of its history and the history of those who have used it over time. Observing these remnants of the past encourages historians to engage themselves in recreating this past function – to rediscover their original purpose and thus explain to modern generations precisely what they are doing there in the landscape. Like the pubs found on trunk roads, many other pubs have developed to serve a different clientele who have taken a break from travelling. Britain is littered with pubs beside canals and rivers that once served the needs of those who were involved in transporting goods by boat or barge all over the country – goods now carried by lorries up and down the motorway network. This has left such pubs to service a tourist trade often in search of a heritage experience which echoes the day before yesterday. Many pubs can also be found close to railway stations, serving a busy clientele catching trains and arriving at their destination. In the UK there are villages that have long since lost their railway stations and their railway lines, yet still preserve their 'Railway Inn'. In others there are 'Station Hotels' and in some villages the unmistakable pub- or hotel-style architecture has been preserved in the fascia of a private house.

Other pubs, through their location, preserve evidence of their past clientele. Some pubs even adapted their offerings especially to accommodate the needs of their clientele outside the conventional licensing hours established by law. London's Covent Garden fruit and vegetable market had a local pub which operated early in the morning to serve the market's porters. It was a similar story further east where the pub nearest London's largest railway junction, in Clapham, had a similar arrangement for railway workers who had finished their night shift.

Individual public houses have names and these frequently preserve important pieces of heritage. In the Celtic fringe it is more common to see public houses named after a past or present owner. Yet, interestingly, a recent variation on this has seen whole chains of pubs adopt a single name as a form of corporate identity. In England most pubs have a name that is also portrayed to its customers with a vivid and memorable sign. The most popular of these names commemorate past monarchs with the title 'King's Head' or 'Queen's Head'. Generally it is possible to look at the pub's sign to see the particular king or queen commemorated.

Portraits of King Henry VII adorn some pubs, whilst Richard III, his opponent at the battle of Bosworth in 1485 which concluded the War of the Roses, is represented in others. It is even possible to trace the resolution of this war through pub signs. Upon the death of King Richard III the two royal houses of York and Lancaster were united into the House of Tudor through Henry VII's marriage to Margaret of York. Both York and Lancaster had different representations of the rose as their symbol; the open white rose for York and the closed red rose for Lancaster. Henry cleverly incorporated facets of both roses to create the symbol of his new dynasty; the amalgamated Tudor Rose. This piece of propaganda is most readily preserved in the popular pub name 'The Rose and Crown'. The symbols of other monarchs quite frequently appear on pub signs as well. The well-known public house name 'The White Hart' uses the emblem of King Richard II, sometimes with other symbols invoking the British monarchy. Overall it is possible to see many of England's kings and queens commemorated in pub signs, although quite clearly some are more popular than others. There may very well be an over-representation of kings and queens who reigned during the last two hundred years. This is useful in reminding us that the evidence that sometimes remains has overwritten an earlier past. Public houses, inns, and taverns have regularly called themselves the 'King's Head' or the 'Queen's Head' but their original, older, establishment may have commemorated an earlier monarch or perhaps several. As time passed, popular feeling, sentiment, and simply the urge to update and renovate a building might have altered the pub sign and thus transformed the monarch commemorated. This famously happened in Leicester around the time of the battle of Bosworth in 1485. Richard III was commemorated in a local market side tavern which was named after his symbol – the White Boar. By the time Richard was defeated, and Leicester was entered by his victorious opponent Henry Tudor, the pub had hurriedly transformed itself into the 'Blue Boar' to escape any taint of disloyalty.

Other public house names similarly commemorate other personalities and events in English history. There are a considerable number of pubs which commemorate Britain's seagoing heritage, with a significant representation of the famous victory at Trafalgar in 1805. While some are named after the battle directly, others commemorate the wider achievements of Admiral Nelson. The land battles of the Napoleonic war are frequently commemorated by the numerous pubs named after the Duke of Wellington. However, sometimes lesser elements in individuals' careers are unwittingly remembered and pub signs can record the false memories of history; many people mistakenly note that the pub name 'The Iron Duke' refers to Wellington's military prowess. In actual fact it commemorates a later incident when he was prime minister and ordered shutters fitted to his London residence to avoid the violence and disdain of the mob calling for parliamentary reform in the 1820s. Posterity has merely mistakenly associated the name with Wellington's military achievements. Other public houses commemorate heroes of wars and sometimes the male and female stars of the nineteenth-century music hall and theatre. Or they may remember political figures such as Lord John Russell, W.E. Gladstone, or Benjamin Disraeli. It is worth reflecting on how these also represent a visible legacy of events that help to add to national memory and tradition, something we encountered in the last chapter.

Some rather different aspects of English social, rather than political, history are also commemorated in other pub names. Some commemorate the name and coat of arms of the local gentry and nobility, often reflecting the fact that the pub concerned was built on the estate of these local families, yet sometimes it is also simply out of deference. Thus it is quite common to find a pub which uses the family name followed by a reference to the coat of arms of the family, which also often finds its way on to the pub sign. Yet there are other coats of arms which appear on pub signs for wholly different reasons. Many of these refer to specific trades such as the 'Brickmakers Arms', the 'Bookbinders Arms', the 'Plasterers Arms', and the 'Carpenters Arms'. In many cases it is quite possible to make distinct connections between the pub's name and the customers who frequented it. Certainly it was common for trades to socialize with one another after work and to use the public house as an informal labour exchange when individuals sought work for themselves. However, the labour in the skilled trades was still more organized than this. The societies which regulated many of these trades had developed quite sophisticated methods of making the labour in those trades mobile enough to ensure all could gain a living. From the middle of the eighteenth century onwards most skilled trades had a 'tramping system'. This subsidized unemployed members of the trade in their search for work, encouraging them to travel a route around the country in search of employment. They were each given a detailed list of the public houses they were to travel to on each stage of the journey. At each of these they would be given a small sum of money and a bed for the night, and inquiry would be made within the locality as to whether there was gainful employment for them. If no such employment could be found, the individual would travel to the next public house mentioned on the tramping circuit list. This would continue until the individual could find employment, or had returned to his original place of origin when hopefully trade conditions had improved.

Public houses were often important places where local branches of friendly societies (the pension and welfare organizations of their age) would convene and transact their business. This reflected the central place of the public house as a venue where individuals could meet and talk with some degree of privacy. Quite often the publican would also sit on the management committee of this organization, very often as treasurer. This reflected local trust in the publican as a significant figure in the local community, but also represented simple convenience since, from a practical point of view, it was easier to handle the society's funds in a public house.

We have branched out from our initial investigation, since from the history of beer and the public house we have found ourselves discussing an aspect of the history of welfare. Yet our investigations can take us further in some different directions emphasizing an interconnected history. Many of these public houses also preserve the history of friendly societies in names such as 'The Foresters' and 'The Oddfellows', which were probably the two most important international organizations based around the friendly society principle. Friendly societies organized insurance and pension schemes operated by labouring men to provide for themselves and their families in adversity. Throughout the world these organizations have met in public houses or eventually gravitated to operating their own clubs which themselves served beer to members and guests.

The public house itself

It is often said that history (rather than archaeology) relies on the use of texts. The written word conveys the actions and motives of the past and forms the bulk of the sources a historian might use. However, since the 1960s, historians have also been more willing to look at buildings, fields, and artefacts as though they were historical texts. Like any text, if we interrogate an inanimate object long enough, it can start to tell us about its history and about the past. Fields viewed from the air can show past farming patterns; the layout of town streets betrays evidence of earlier settlements. If we start to investigate buildings we can see the legacy of history and past usage in the plans and layout of many different kinds of premises. The interior layout of the public house has altered dramatically throughout the twentieth century, but there was a marked acceleration of this trend in the last twenty years of the century. The changing use and layout of buildings not only tells us the history of those individual buildings, but can also point to wider social and economic changes in history. Many public houses in the modern world are one-bar establishments where all customers have their requirements catered for within a multi-purpose and flexible environment. But it was not always this way. If we look closely we can still see some of the evidence that, in the past, the public house performed a variety of functions and fulfilled a great number of needs within the community. This history is reconstructed by looking at the architectural heritage and history of public houses.

It is still possible to see the remnants of these functions in public house architecture that remains. Some pubs have their bar jutting out from the back of the premises, filling the centre of the building's area. This so-called 'island' bar arrangement was invented by the engineer Isambard Kingdom Brunel as a method of enabling public houses to cope with a sudden influx of customers deposited at destinations by the railway – a new phenomenon in its age. This tells us about the consumption patterns of the past, whereby drinking beer was considered both reviving and the gateway to leisure time after work. Leisure was another comparatively recent nineteenth-century invention which had an increasingly symbiotic relationship with the railway.

Other parts of the public house tell us other stories. It is too easily forgotten that in earlier centuries the public house was a source of heat and light in communities that often had a considerable shortage of both of these. Thus all were drawn to the premises and it was common before the 1960s, and sometimes even later than this, for pubs to be divided into a public bar and a saloon bar. In a way this allowed pubs to be all-purpose centres for the community and to reflect social differences that originated outside the drinking establishment itself. This bar arrangement allowed foremen and managers to drink separately from their workforce. This was generally reflected in the lower cost of beer in the public bar. The saloon bar was also generally the preserve of women customers or couples enjoying their leisure time. In many respects the disappearance of these two areas leads us into an historical consideration of the social changes that have seen class distinctions marginalized, whilst expectations about women's use of public space have similarly altered almost beyond recognition.

We can also see that other rooms within the average public house building have likewise disappeared. The so-called 'smoke room' has fallen foul of changing attitudes to health and smoking as an acceptable public phenomenon. Many public houses also had a separate area for selling beer and other drinks for home consumption. Often quaintly called the 'jug and bottle', this area was frequently segregated from the rest of the pub, thereby allowing children to enter the public house to buy sweets, crisps, and soft drinks. The antiquated title of this area is far removed from the manner in which take-away beer (and sweets, crisps, and soft drinks for that matter) are all purchased today. Most pubs' 'jug and bottle' bars have fallen victim to the corner shop and supermarket. These other outlets have economies of scale in purchasing that offer cost advantages to customers, as well as greater convenience with the spread of longer opening hours well into the night. Other public houses used to have intimate 'snug rooms' where courting couples could retire for a discreet cuddle and kiss. These have long since fallen into disuse with the growing liberal attitudes to premarital relationships, alongside more comfortable and less crowded housing where courtship has been relocated.

Whilst pubs used to have games rooms and outdoor arrangements, sometimes devoted to local sports such as skittles, bowls, or Aunt Sally, their gradual disappearance has not wholly led to the end of pub games. Some native pub games, such as bar billiards, have been replaced by the American import of pool. Whilst darts retains a significant following in both Britain and America, both are more likely to be set to one side in a one-bar pub. Moreover the influx of global media money into coverage of sport has encouraged the more passive consumption of high-level sport through the arrival of large television screens in many pubs and bars around the world. This interrogation of the pub building is something the historian can do with other premises such as churches, municipal buildings, and even houses. These all betray the intention of those who built them and those who subsequently have used them from that day to this.

Ordering a beer: but what type of beer?

Several different styles of beer actually contain small pieces of history and heritage and these often tell us quite a lot about the people who drank them in the past, as the consumption of any other commodity might. The dark beer with a creamy head called porter was so named because it was the favourite drink of market porters in London. Until recently in public houses in the Midlands and the south-east of England it was possible to drink a beer called mild. This was a dark beer which was fruity and flavoursome but was quite low in strength compared to many other beers both then and now. This beer originated in the West Midlands in the so-called 'Black Country' where the smelting of iron and the production of other metal goods was the area's main industry. Mild was designed for workers from these hot and sweaty industries to slake their thirst quickly and cheaply without becoming intoxicated. Some of the more common brown beers also have evocative names that betray their past. Several bitter beers are known as IPAs, which is an abbreviation which stands for India Pale Ale. These beers were middle strength so that drinking them in very hot climates was not an uncomfortable experience, yet they were also sufficiently strong to be able to survive the journey by boat to the Indian subcontinent. These IPAs can be found in England and Scotland, but are also brewed by local breweries as far away as Australia, Sweden, and the USA. Most pale lager beers are generally referred to as 'Pilsners' and this commemorates their invention in the town of Pilsen in what was then Bohemia. Some of the names, or rather designations of beer, also reflect important parts of the past. Many beers have a number of 'X's listed after their name and this reflects Europe's long history of brewing in monasteries. This 'X' designation indicated the strength of the beer by the number of letters used after its name or marked on the barrel. Interestingly we can find other remnants of monastic brewing in a number of continental European beers collectively known under the name of 'Trappist' – after the order of monks who perfected them. Other beers sometimes have a monetary amount expressed in pre-decimal currency such as 50/- or 80/-, reflecting the cost of the barrel of the beer described in the distant past. Naturally enough, the more expensive the beer, the stronger it was. This connects beer with the industrial past, with empire, and with the medieval monastery here functioning as a centre of both learning and industry.

The tradition of brewing has followed human migration across the world, and sometimes simply the act of standing in a bar and being confronted by the evidence of this can be overwhelming for the historian experiencing an encounter with the traditions and heritage of another country. This is especially true in America, where the variety of beers available shows us the indelible footprint of America's past as a refuge from Europe. America reflects the brewing traditions of many countries, with Pilsner- and Bock-style beers reflecting the heritage of German immigrants. Similarly Irish red beers and stouts echo the thousands who sailed to America both before and after the potato famine of 1846. Scottish 'heavies' again reflect the tastes of immigrants, as do Danish- and Scandinavian-style lagers.

Sometimes the exotic and interesting names of the beers themselves, and the way they are portrayed on bottles and hand pumps, are an important story in themselves, conveying the history of significant attitudes, feelings, and ideas to the beer consumer. Some reflect famous historical events, local dignitaries, or local historical heroes. One porter originating from Suffolk commemorates the activities of Matthew Hopkins, the infamous 'Witch Finder General', whose activities resulted in the trial, prosecution, and execution of a number of witches in the area during the mid-1640s. Some reflect elements of local identity that speak of a fiercely proud local tradition and attitude. The famous brown ale from Newcastle has on its label a depiction of the local landmark the Tyne Bridge, whilst one of London's leading breweries self-consciously entitles its bitter beer 'London Pride'. Some other beers go for a readily identifiable image of their country of origin. At least two breweries in England in the recent past used the image of a field sportsman in full hunting regalia as an unmistakable image of rural England. Some beers' names have been known to commemorate the importance of certain trades, with a beer entitled 'Tanner's Jack' commemorating the leather trade of the Home Counties. Similarly a brewery in Norfolk named its bitter beer 'Norfolk Wherry' to celebrate the coastal barge trade that brought goods to and from East Anglia carried in barges particular to the region, called 'Wherries'.

Frequently it is even possible to note that a beer's quality is guaranteed by the heritage behind it. Many German beers state on the serving tap, or on the bottle or can, that the production methods used and the ingredients involved adhere to laws of considerable antiquity. The German Reinheitsgebot (or law of purity) first appeared at the end of the fifteenth century in Bavaria but was properly codified in 1516. This law originally specified the ingredients that were to be used, limiting them to malted barley, water, and hops. This law also regulated the cost of beer, which suggests how important it was as a part of the diet, and arguably a central part of life, in sixteenth-century Europe. This law governed the production of beer until it was amended in the early 1990s to allow other ingredients, such as wheat and cane sugar, to be used in beer production. Interestingly many German breweries still refer to the fact that production methods adhere to this original law – the Reinheitsgebot. This cleverly associates them with nearly five hundred years of brewing tradition, giving their customers a glow of satisfaction that they are drinking a beverage supposedly unaltered since the early modern period.

Occasionally this emotion can crop up in the unlikeliest of places – or at least they appear to be unlikely until we remember the heritage and the history. In South Africa one of the nicest lager beers declares on its label that it is brewed according to the Reinheitsgebot which, at first sight, seems something of a mystery. The mystery deepens when it is suggested by advertising in the bar that you have a small glass of fruit-flavoured schnapps to go with your beer. Yet a closer look at the label tells us that the beer was brewed in Windhoek (now in modern Namibia) which was originally part of German South-West Africa, clearly suggesting how brewing practice followed colonialism out of Europe and into the new worlds. This story is replicated in China since the beer named Tsingtao emanates from what was the most significant German colony on the Chinese mainland, before its capture by the Japanese during the First World War.

Beer and heritage: the invention of tradition

Given the devotion to heritage and history by brewers, publicans, and even the public at large, it is also possible to be persuaded of false and sometimes damaging histories. Some of the tradition and antiquity on display may not always be what it seems. Something that appears to have a long heritage and history may, in reality, have appeared overnight or have been engineered to appear considerably older than it actually is. Historians call this the 'invention of tradition' and have noted how this desire to provide a constructed artificial past provides a legitimacy and tradition for something, aiding its acceptance by those who think about its nature and origins. This phenomenon was noted by the historians Terence Ranger and Eric Hobsbawm. They both looked to the considerable range of historical examples where a tradition, supposedly going back hundreds of years, was actually of much more recent origin. They noted, for example, how the antiquity of the Scottish kilt, and the family tartans emblazoned on it, could in reality only be traced back as far as the middle of the nineteenth century. They were even bold enough to tie this invention explicitly to a single event, the visit of Queen Victoria to Scotland in the middle of the nineteenth century. Victoria and Albert were the celebrity couple of early nineteenth-century England; associating an invented tradition with them was seen by some entrepreneurial Scots as sealing the success of the venture of actively constructed heritage.

Similarly, we might come to distrust the number of beers whose names begin with the prefix 'old'. Some may genuinely be as old as they claim, yet others may merely reflect the use of an old recipe known to the brewery or dredged up from the mists of time. Occasionally when breweries amalgamate or merge they might acquire the names and brewing portfolios of another company. Sometimes the name can actually vanish for years, only to find itself suddenly resurrected in an 'invention of tradition'. In the early 1990s a particular Irish bitter was advertised on British television. The advert showed a man entering a bar somewhere in America where he asked for one of these beers. Immediately the bar dissolved into a depiction of an imagined Ireland. He walked past a group of men returning from playing hurling, a distressed-looking fishing boat, and a bright-eyed and beautiful colleen. All this gave this beer an instant association with a nostalgic Ireland, unwisely left behind by the unfortunate man in America. Yet although this was a brand from the past, before the early 1990s, the English Campaign for Real Ale drew everyone's attention to the fact that the brewery had not brewed beer since the end of the Edwardian period. This heritage had been explicitly invented for this advert.

Although the advert concealed the truth about the origin of this beer, it perhaps also told a lie that was greater still. The Ireland that immigrants left in their thousands since the eighteenth century was not always the happy, contented place depicted in the advert. Religious bigotry against both Catholics and Presbyterians, famine, and poor employment prospects forced many to leave for America. So the historian must always be discerning about the created image of the past, be alive to how it is used, and aim to explore and explain the truth or lies that it tells. Likewise the historian must always be wary of attempts to create a mythical golden age intended to encourage and enrich modern consumption. The creation of such myths is about marketing far more than it is about history, which remains a search for the truth.

Equally the rise of the theme pub is also quite often an exercise in the further 'invention of tradition'. Even the simple act of hanging a sepia-stained photograph on the wall is arguably pandering to the 'invention of tradition'. Again we might note the rise of the Irish (and in Sweden the rise of the English) theme pub as an example of this phenomenon. Many of these contain adverts for products from the first half of the twentieth century displayed on the wall. Quite often they might also have pre-distressed furniture and fittings, all intended to convey years of use and a cosy antiquity. This is to make drinkers feel at ease and to persuade them, as before, that they follow in the steps of previous generations.

Heritage and tradition: what is the historian's task?

Historical investigations can begin from the simplest and humblest starting point and can take the investigator in some surprising directions. Humble starting points have so often led professional and amateur historians alike deeply into their enthusiasm for the past. The historian's job is to uncover the truth and to be able to discern tradition from its invention. But equally in seeking to uncover the truth about the mundane history around us, the historian becomes a curator of the past's legacy. This places the responsibility on the historian to be a custodian of heritage, so that the mundane things as well as the great men and women of history may have a part in a nation's or community's heritage and history. It is the purpose of the historian as far as possible to be involved in the cataloguing, conservation, protection, and importance of the heritage that they find. We may not be able to save everything in a modernizing and changing world, but the historian is capable of helping to decide what is important and worth saving. Some of the remnants I have described in this chapter, like all heritage, are constantly under threat or in danger of disappearing. Some may even have disappeared whilst I have been writing this chapter. This should make all interested in history realize that it is sometimes missionary work – the act of cataloguing and recording the memory of the past before it is lost and gone forever.

6

Changing histories – informing the past and thinking about the future

A great many people think that they already 'know' important areas of the history that matters to them. That is, they have accepted a plausible explanation of an important historical event or phenomenon and are broadly happy with this established version of events. This generally occurs because historians are in the business of providing explanations for these historical events. Explanations gain credibility because historians endorse them. They do this because they are familiar with the subject area and the historical sources. They also invariably use their judgement about the most likely explanation being the correct one. As we have learned, this is based on the quest for objectivity and the search for explanations that embrace and demonstrate our tests of credibility, likelihood, and verifiability.

Yet we do need to look closely at how the telling of history changes and how this enables us to alter our understanding of history and how it happened. What happens when, for example, something drastic occurs and the orthodox version of a historical phenomenon or event is changed utterly as a result of new developments? Inevitably our accepted picture of history changes and it is an important reminder that historical explanations and interpretations are seldom final. If this were the case then history would cease to be written and cease to be altered. So how does this type of change occur? Historians invariably approach subjects with their own different perspectives and these are sometimes acquired as a result of experience, ethnicity, gender, or other forms of identity. Occasionally ideological inclination can influence the explanation an historian might offer. Sometimes changes in the availability of sources themselves might mean that our picture of a specific event or phenomenon is changed completely by new material, to which a previous generation of historians simply did not have access. Sometimes it is about adopting new approaches which bring together previously known sources that had not been brought together before. Sometimes change can occur as a result of scholars bringing their knowledge of other disciplines to an accepted historical interpretation. All these factors can change our perception of the history we thought we already knew.

When early twentieth-century archaeologists tried to explain the supplanting of one ancient civilization by another, they were often instinctively interested in excavating battlefields, because the ancient history that they knew had concentrated on this aspect of life. These historical events had been central to the classics of ancient literature, such as the work of Tacitus we met in the second chapter. In other words they were steered by their existing knowledge and the assumptions this knowledge gave them. Thus, it was no surprise that their explanations of how one culture supplanted another were based entirely on conquest – one culture was driven out by the conquering agenda of another. However, in the later twentieth century archaeologists looked beyond the traditional battlefields to excavate settlements, dwellings, sites of industry, and trading posts. The results from these led to a challenge to the conquest model of how civilizations come and go. Instead, looking at these new sources told archaeologists that there was much more evidence of new civilizations spreading their influence through trade, exchange of information, and eventually intermarriage over a much longer period than the alleged abrupt change wrought by a decisive battle. This process became known as 'acculturation' and eventually became the dominant explanation of how civilizations were supplanted – so much so that those who argue for the decisiveness of battles in the process today find themselves swimming against the tide of opinion. This demonstrates how one view of history was created by the assumptions of one group of historians relying on what they considered to be the sources available. Yet their views were supplanted by succeeding groups with the very opposite interests and assumptions, fuelled by the examination of different evidence. It is also important to bear in mind the influence of lived experience on these two groups of historians. The first group, those who believed in the conquest explanation, had lived through a century and a half in which war had repeatedly altered the map of Europe and other parts of the world. Those in the second group, people advocating the 'acculturation' explanation, had seen the years since the Second World War demonstrate the benefits of co-operation, trade agreements, and the United Nations. They may even have been convinced that the fall of the Eastern Bloc was itself a process of 'acculturation' in which the virtues of Western democracy had stealthily supplanted communism. In their own minds, they had seen the process of 'acculturation' play out in their own contemporary history and it became easy to imagine this equally happening in a past context.

The abolition of the slave trade: humanitarian act or self-interest? Historians debate the power of different explanations

The year 2007 gave the historical profession not only the opportunity to re-appraise the history of the slave trade, but also to consider the event of its abolition which celebrated its two-hundredth anniversary in that year. Very obviously the idea of the slave trade is an emotive one and it is scarcely surprising that it has constituted a battleground for those touched by history and its importance. It is very clearly a history of exploitation, a history of suffering, and a history where the power of the strong was used to subjugate the weak. It is also a history of sites where the very nature of civilization itself seems to be contested. How could supposedly civilized countries like Britain, France, Portugal, and the American Colonies involve themselves in the traffic of human misery for gain? Black Africans were systematically captured, traded, and subsequently enslaved on Caribbean plantations, where their sole purpose in life was to produce sugar for the tea tables of Western Europe. Certainly histories of slavery have now been produced to take into account and give voice to the downtrodden slave as part of a wider mission to include the voices of those who had previously been hidden from history. Thus the lives of slave men and slave women give an account of this history from the point of view of the enslaved, sometimes in the form of histories of slave rebellion. These voices have underlined that the practice was scarcely routinely accepted by a meek, broken, and downtrodden community. But, as we have suggested, the purpose of history is to explain and analyse as much as it is to catalogue and elaborate on earlier historical accounts and writings. One of the most important things any history of slavery has had to do has been to explain how and why the slave trade was ended by the British parliament in 1807 and how it came to be completely outlawed in 1833. These explanations in their various forms have also had a particularly political flavour, with attempts to apportion blame and to exonerate nations, races, and interest groups inevitably tied up in the course and direction of the different explanations.

For much of the first half of the twentieth century the abolition of the slave trade in Britain was explained through reference to a growing sense of philanthropy blended with an awakening of religious consciousness and conscience. It was argued that in the late eighteenth century people were beginning to realize that slavery belonged to a more barbaric and less enlightened age. It had been considered thoroughly acceptable in the sixteenth and seventeenth centuries, but at some point in the eighteenth attitudes towards this changed. From this point onwards the influence of evangelical religion promoted a greater awareness of humanitarian duties to one's fellow men and women. The rise of Methodism and the influence this had on other forms of evangelicalism persuaded people, through this new piety, that trafficking and trading in slaves was inhumane and ungodly. Therefore, the evil system that supported this should be brought down. Chief among these was William Wilberforce who personified this evangelical awakening of conscience. He campaigned tirelessly throughout the country, fighting for the cause of abolition, and his reputation spread as far as the West Indies where the slaves referred to him as 'St Wilforce'. Eventually, so this traditional account had it, the overwhelming tide of moral indignation wore Parliament down and it was eventually persuaded to concede the abolition of the slave trade in 1807, and finally the end of slavery itself in 1833.

However, for historians it is important to note that the reception of explanations can also be governed by attitudes reflecting the contemporary world and its pre-occupations. It is worth noting from the outset that this particular explanation of the ending of the slave trade was convenient on a whole range of levels. It was very much a white, English (and to an extent male) explanation which suited the story early twentieth-century British society wished to tell itself. This was a country that had presided over a vast and impressive empire, but this was entering its twilight years. This growing discomfort about the whole issue of imperial possession and colonial rule was to lead to Britain establishing self-government in almost all of its colonies by the middle of the twentieth century. A story that spoke of a growing tide of benevolence that removed barbaric practices suited a country which was in the midst of going through a similar process of modernization. This would remove the supposed barbaric behaviour of empire from the British consciousness of the recent past. This was one important reason that this early explanation of the abolition of the slave trade was based on the idea of a philanthropic impulse.

This explanation was altered fundamentally by the publication, in 1944, of a book which challenged this interpretation from its top to its very bottom. So revolutionary were the implications of this new theory that it significantly altered the politics of this particular historical event. The theory reached from the past it sought to discuss to influence the present by affecting the lives of individuals and the images people had of their own past. The author was a black West Indian named Eric Williams who had left his native Trinidad to take up a scholarship at Oxford University in 1932. As a historian Williams himself had influences and agendas in writing his history, every bit as much as those who apologized for Britain in its fading imperial years. Williams grew up alongside the ideas of Marcus Garvey, who founded the Universal Negro Improvement Association arguing for a discovery of black Afro-Caribbean identity. These were assertive Black Nationalist ideas and were augmented by the fact that Williams was taught by an influential black Marxist historian, C.L.R. James. Thus he was persuaded by Black Nationalism and Marxism, what we might call historical theories, that he should write an alternative history.

This combination of influences persuaded Williams to think differently about the accepted history of slavery abolition. Unconvinced by the conventional interpretation of slavery that he found in 1930s Oxford, his own theoretical inheritance and research led him in a fundamentally different direction. This resulted in a book entitled *Capitalism and Slavery* which offered a vastly different interpretation, so far-reaching that it arguably spoke to issues and historical incidents beyond slavery.

Anxious to deprive the English of the moral high ground and to assert a Marxist explanation, he argued that slavery had in fact come to an end for economic rather than philosophical reasons. His book did not talk simply about the issue of repeal, but instead sketched the history of a whole system of oppression and the imperatives that operated it. This logically stemmed from Williams failing to accept the simple argument that altruism ended slavery. As a historian he saw that understanding this system of oppression was important for explaining the cause and circumstances of its downfall, and for comprehending the big picture drawn from the theory that he was sketching.

He began by showing how the system of colonial plantations had evolved in large-scale units which almost inevitably led to the use of slave labour. According to this theory, slavery became an economic phenomenon as much as it was connected with the subjugation of one race by another. As Williams argued:

> Slavery in the Caribbean has been too narrowly identified with the Negro. A racial twist has thereby been given to what is basically an economic phenomenon. Slavery was not born of racism: rather, racism was the consequence of slavery. Unfree labour in the new world was brown, white, black, and yellow; catholic, protestant and pagan.

This focus on economics was also important for making his audience realize that the slave trade was only one part of a wider, astoundingly profitable, commercial system. This was a three-cornered traffic known as the 'Triangular Trade' and there is no better description of it than the one Williams himself gave:

> This Triangular Trade – England, France and colonial America equally – supplied the exports and the ships; Africa the human merchandise; the plantations the colonial raw materials. The slave ship sailed from the home country with a cargo of manufactured goods. These were exchanged at a profit on the coast of Africa for Negroes, who were traded

on the plantations, at another profit, in exchange for a cargo of colonial produce to be taken back to the home country. As the volume of trade increased, the triangular trade was supplemented, but never supplanted, by a direct trade between home country and the West Indies, exchanging home manufactures directly for colonial produce.

However, within this trading system there was one factor which was eventually to prove its Achilles heel. All Caribbean sugar and cotton was to be traded with the home country and this trade was to be restricted to being carried in British shipping. Similarly, these colonies were to buy their goods and services solely from British suppliers. Eighteenth-century economic thinkers argued that tying them into a monopoly would benefit all concerned in these trades, but especially the mother country. Williams went on to argue that England's own textile industries came to the fringe of what was to become their later dominant position as a result of supplying the triangular trade. Wool and cotton clothes were needed in the West Indies to clothe the vast slave populations, whilst in return plantations in these colonies supplied half of England's stock of raw cotton in 1764. The system sketched by Williams extended as far as the spades and tools necessary for the cultivation of sugar which were virtually all manufactured in Birmingham. The chain-making industry in the West Midlands 'Black Country' also grew prosperous as a result of the demand for restraints, chains, padlocks, and branding irons – all gruesome tools for the enforcement and operation of slavery. These metallurgical industries also produced other material and finished goods that were traded on the West African coast for slaves.

Eric Williams constructed for his readers a social system built on these flourishing economic interests. With all these economic interests interwoven, it is no surprise that individuals who embodied the West Indian interest were extremely powerful members of society. They were extremely well represented in both Houses of Parliament in England and their influence was particularly strong in an age where patronage and connection were the keys to political power. But Williams was also careful to argue that it was not simply the manufacturing and commercial sectors that benefited from slavery and the triangular trade. Britain's modern banking system emerged through its involvement in financing both slavery and the triangular trade in Liverpool, Glasgow, and Bristol. The most notable of these bankers were David and Alexander Barclay whose descendants founded the modern Barclays bank. The demands of the West Indian colonies importantly also touched other sectors of the economy beyond manufacturing in some almost forgotten areas. The Atlantic fishing industry owed some of its prosperity to the need to provide fish capable of being preserved for the long voyage to Africa and across the Atlantic. Likewise Ireland was practically turned into one large market garden producing cash crops for export to these West Indian colonies. The logic of this market-driven economics was also an essential part of the Marxist message that Williams wanted to convey. Slavery made profit and the market forces this exerted on the rest of the economy made Ireland a market garden and Britain into a centre of manufacturing. This produced social change on the back of economic change, as predicted by Marx.

But Eric Williams had not spent the bulk of his book constructing the history of this system without having a wider intention and another important story to tell, which would change our historical perceptions. He had never lost sight of the need to provide an explanation for the abolition of the slave trade and of slavery itself. What he argued was that this self-perpetuating system, built on the eighteenth century's economic thinking and trading patterns, began to fall apart as, one by one, significant interest groups turned against it. This was also a way of saying that the system was so strong, and had existed with such impeccable logic, that only a change in that logic could bring about its downfall.

The first brick to be removed from this edifice was the issue of the sugar monopoly. New manufacturing interests wished to reduce the cost of basic foodstuffs (in this case bread and sugar). This was because they wished to lower the wages they paid to their own workers. Sugar refiners desperately wanted relief from the West Indian monopoly over their raw material to make their exports cheaper in European markets. Similarly towns that had benefited from the slave and sugar trades were no longer prepared to support these trades when their own interests had changed. Liverpool turned away from its economic dependence on sugar and the slave trade to become the port where the growing Lancashire cotton industry imported its raw material.

All these contrived to bring down an economic system that was no longer fit for the age in which it was still clinging on – the situation had dramatically altered and now its time was up. Eric Williams summed this process up in the following words:

> These economic changes are gradual, imperceptible, but they have an irresistible cumulative effect. Men, pursuing their interests, are rarely aware of the ultimate results of their activity. The commercial capitalism of the eighteenth century developed the wealth of Europe by means of slavery and monopoly. But in so doing it helped to create the industrial capitalism of the nineteenth century, which turned around and destroyed the power of commercial capitalism, slavery, and its entire works. Without a grasp of these economic changes the history of the period is meaningless.

The phrase in this quotation 'men pursuing their interests' also leads us to think wider and further about how some of these economic forces can act like ripples across a vast pond. The search for more profitable forms of agriculture meant that people were turned off their land in Scotland so that wool could be produced for foreign markets, such as the West Indies. Similarly the fact that Ireland was an agricultural producer for the West Indies left its population vulnerable to the demographic disaster that was the 1846 potato famine. Together these migrants, Scots and Irish, carried with them a hunger for land that would in turn have its impact on the indigenous peoples of America, Canada, Australia, South Africa, and New Zealand.

Eric Williams and his ideas were scarcely popular within the historical profession of his day, since they placed the historical voice of the Caribbean in opposition to that of the English historical establishment. Williams, however, went on to a much more exalted position as Prime Minister of Trinidad and Tobago, an office he held for twenty years until his death in 1981. To this day his historical work on the system of slavery, its implications, and its downfall remains current and relevant. Moreover for our purposes it demonstrates how a single historian, operating differently to those who had gone before, can change our historical perception of an event or phenomenon. Williams's upbringing and his ideas brought a profoundly new perspective to an established historical explanation. But likewise his explanation was not the end of the story. As more historical investigations were pursued, Williams's own theories came under scrutiny and some elements of his argument were partially challenged. Roger Anstey suggested in 1968 that Williams overestimated the decline in the profitability of slavery, arguing that it was still more than viable on the eve of its abolition. Joel Mokyr, writing in 1993, doubted the idea that the profits from slavery fuelled the industrial revolution and instead argued that these found their way back to the Caribbean plantations.

Perhaps it seems a little alarming to see how these two different historical interpretations of the slave trade and its abolition appeared to turn around individuals with vested interests – or what in less charitable moments we might seek to call 'axes to grind'. At first sight this might persuade the reader that such interpretations are not valid – historians after all ought to seek to tell the truth, irrespective of whether this suits them or fits any agenda that they are trying to justify. However, this particular example demonstrates that history is never written in a vacuum. We are all products of our age and its concerns, as well as the products of our own prejudices.

Moreover historians have a right to think that their views on the reality of what happened in history, and why, should change our view about society just as much as any other member of the population. So if they seek to do this through the history they are writing, they are perhaps no different to any other member of the human race. But equally this situation does not simply need to be explained away. If historians do have agendas and if they do confront previous history with these, this is an important reminder of how history is regularly contested, why it is contested, and probably why it should always be contested. Williams challenged existing theories based on evidence, and eventually his own theories have been challenged based on counter-evidence. This is also a reminder of how history is written to address and galvanize a contemporary society into action as much as it is a reminder of a past society. As such the theories historians create through speaking about the past also speak viably to the present. Sometimes the power of such theories to explain phenomena in the past become seductive and persuade commentators that the lessons of the past might hold extremely valuable keys to the future. The next section illustrates an example of how and why this happens – together with the problems this causes for the historian and sometimes those who consume this history.

Creating theories and predictions: why empires rise and fall

One aspect of making sense of the past is to create cyclical theories about how and why events or changes occurred in the historical past and how these potentially happen more than once to establish a pattern. In many respects this is the most potent and effective way to satisfy the historian's desire to know why something happened. Using this method offers the chance to provide deeper and lasting explanations of how things happened in the past. Why did certain things happen when they did? Why did an individual pursue one course of action rather than another? Why did the dominance of one area of life/society/ the world eclipse that of another? And last of all, can we see a pattern in these changes that may help us to explain a number of similar instances? These are all questions which historians can try to answer with the use of theory. Yet one thing that changes the value of such theories is how they can be challenged by subsequent events, or by new perspectives on the theory itself. Moreover, if we do have a theory that explains a number of historical occurrences, there is a temptation to consider using it to think about the contemporary world.

We can observe the construction of such a theory and its use right up to the present day by following the development of the ideas of the historian Paul Kennedy, and his attempt to offer an explanation for how powerful empires had grown and dissolved throughout history. In his early years as an academic he produced books with titles such as *The Realities Behind Diplomacy*, *The Rise of British Naval Mastery*, and *The Rise of Anglo-German Antagonism*. These brought his ideas to the attention of a scholarly but also a popular reading public.

During the mid-1980s Paul Kennedy worked on his next book *The Rise and Fall of the Great Powers* (published in 1987). Once again this book was filled with rousing stories, but again also had at its root a deceptively simple idea. Kennedy argued that if historians looked closely at a number of different empires throughout history, they would see that these empires' growth and development followed an almost inevitable pattern. The initial impetus behind an empire would be swiftly followed by dramatic growth and commensurate wealth and prestige for the home country of an imperial nation. However, with such growth in size and territory came a considerable growth in commitments. Empires needed defending from jealous predators and from various local groups and dissidents prepared to throw off the yoke of imperial rule. This involved the increasing commitment of military technology and manpower that inevitably did not come cheap. Such defences and protection invariably required financial support which would be a burden borne by the empire's taxpayers. Kennedy argued that this burden grew significantly over time, as his historical examples could show. Under this burden, commerce suffered and empires eventually ran out of money to fund the defence of their far-flung colonies and dependent territories. This became known from his work as the 'over-extension thesis'.

Once again it was based on a comparatively simple idea – if any nation was able to acquire an empire, then eventually the cost of maintaining it would become too great a burden to bear. Moreover Kennedy could produce plenty of examples that illustrated his theory, and many of the historical facts seemed to fit his explanation. He looked at a number of empires in turn (the Spanish Habsburg Empire of the sixteenth century, the Dutch Seaborne Empire of the seventeenth century, and the British Empire of the nineteenth/twentieth centuries) and explained their meteoric rise, consolidation, and eventual decline. It was an aim of the book to pinpoint the moments at which the balance swung away from imperial powers, leading them into a situation of almost inevitable decline. At the heart of Kennedy's analysis was the relationship between economics and military power. He strongly suggested that as aspects of a nation's economy changed, this affected this nation's position in the world in relation to other nations. From this he argued that a nation only really became an imperial great power when it became an important military power. This was in turn linked to the outcome of major geopolitical struggles. In short, Kennedy argued what seemed to be obvious to most people – national alliances that could amass the most resources behind them tended to win the wars in which they were frequently engaged.

Although he never argued that his theory worked for all time, his contention was still a bold one, as he analysed the growth of imperial alliances since the year 1500. He commenced this analysis by looking at the Spanish Habsburg Empire which he saw as a classic case of his idea of 'over-extension'. It had been united in the early years of the sixteenth century and eventually found itself the victim of its geography and the circumstances it had created. Warfare had also become phenomenally expensive, with the cost of fortifications and more sophisticated armaments taking its toll on a country that Kennedy pointedly noticed had not even properly organized the collection of taxes. He argued:

> The Habsburgs simply had too much to do, too many empires to fight, too many fronts to defend. The stalwartness of the Spanish troops in battle could not compensate for the fact that these forces had to be dispersed, in homeland garrisons, in North Africa, in Sicily and Italy, and in the New World, as well as in the Netherlands. Like the British Empire three centuries later, the Habsburg bloc was a conglomeration of widely scattered territories, a political dynastic *tour de force* which required enormous sustained resources of material and ingenuity to keep going. As such, it provides one of the greatest examples of strategic overstretch in history; for the price of possessing so many territories was the existence of numerous foes.

Kennedy also argued that the Habsburg Empire could not find acceptable political reasons for withdrawing from fighting on any of these fronts. Indeed, as a small hint about what was to come later in the book, he suggested the Habsburgs thought in terms of their own conception of a 'domino theory'. Thus, their fear that one territory would fall to their enemies fed the further concern that others would follow suit, resulting in the total collapse of their empire.

The argument then charted the rise of the empire of the United Provinces (the modern Netherlands), which grew in confidence after it had successfully withstood the military might of the Habsburg Empire. It grew wealthy through trade and an increasingly sophisticated banking system prepared to invest in an important seaborne empire. This fell into decline when the cost of defending the United Provinces against France, and its territorial ambitions, made the Dutch largely dependent on British sea power and subsidies. By the last third of the eighteenth century the Dutch United Provinces were at the mercy of the French and the British alternately. The French monarchy, its revolutionary armies, and eventually its armies under Napoleon constituted yet a further example of overstretch. Its dramatic demise occurred when confronted by more economically powerful and better-resourced nations who combined in alliance against it. This in turn led to the rise of the British Empire, sometimes built on territories scavenged from the declining French Empire. Kennedy imagined how Napoleon himself must have viewed this process:

> Despite his own assumptions of grandeur, Napoleon seems to have become obsessed with Britain at times – with its invulnerability, its maritime dominance, its banks and credit system – and to have yearned to see it all tumble in the dust. Such feelings of envy and dislike doubtless existed, if in a less extreme form, among the Spaniards, Dutch, and others who saw the British monopolising the outside world.

This empire was then charted as surviving into the twentieth century, when it needed significant help to weather the storms of two World Wars and its eventual withdrawal from many of its colonies overseas. This left Britain as the last historical example of imperial 'over-extension' in the book. The demise of Britain's empire and the rise of the United States as the premiere world power was described thus by Kennedy:

> Given the extraordinarily favourable economic and strategic position which the United States thus occupied, its post-1945 outward thrust could come as no surprise to those familiar with the history of international politics. With the traditional Great Powers fading away, it steadily moved into the vacuum which their going created; having become number one, it could no longer contain itself within its own shores, or even its own hemisphere.

This book followed in the tradition of Kennedy's earlier works that engaged the attention of historians and other readers interested in the history of military strategy and empire. However, Kennedy had one last trick up his sleeve. The book, which was completed in the late 1980s, included a final chapter taking the story up to the year 2000. This stunned readers with a series of educated guesses based on what had happened to the past empires previously described in the book. This ostensibly argued that Russia would fall into a decline, but Kennedy's bombshell asserted that the USA was going the way of the previous empires described and would thus find itself the twenty-first century's first casualty of the 'over-extension' thesis. Although he was anxious to suggest that all was not yet lost, he spoke quite plainly about the difficult tasks that clearly lay ahead for future American governments.

> The task facing American statesmen over the next decades, therefore, is to recognise that broad trends are underway, and that there is a need to 'manage' affairs so that the

relative erosion of the United States' position takes place slowly and smoothly, and is not accelerated by policies which bring merely short term advantage but longer term disadvantage. This involves, from the president's office downward, an appreciation that technological and therefore socioeconomic change is occurring in the world faster than ever before; that the international community is much more politically and culturally diverse than has been assumed, and is defiant of simplistic remedies offered either by Washington or Moscow to its problems.

This attempt to predict the future was a bold move for a historian. Quite often the historical profession shies away from the idea of speculating about future developments, because doing so entails a lot of guesswork. It also tends to involve the historian relying heavily on the theory they have evolved, or the theories created by others. In other words, for a historian, predicting the future entails degrees of risk and an uneasy feeling that the history he or she has written is sometimes being misused. It would of course be nice to predict the future. However, what happened to Paul Kennedy and his ideas from *The Rise and Fall of the Great Powers* illustrates the problems that exist in trying to use history and theories derived from it to investigate the future.

When the book hit the bookshops, it sold in vast numbers that turned the volume rapidly into an international blockbuster. Such success was aided by several reviews which highlighted the implications of the last chapter. This meant that Kennedy's book, for a time, almost ceased to be a history book, and instead began to be seen as a foreign policy primer and advice book. Thus one newspaper suggested Kennedy's *Rise and Fall of the Great Powers* was *the* book to be seen reading if you worked on Capitol Hill. On 15 February 1988 *Time* magazine carried a review of the book, already noting its topicality. It declared that *Rise and Fall of the Great Powers* was:

a new volume that US policymakers and pundits are lugging around in their briefcases, an immense academic history bristling with tables, maps and charts, plus 83 pages of closely printed footnotes and a bibliography that cites nearly 1,400 sources.

At the time the book appeared to be unanswerable in its logic. The past had seen global empires come and go and there was no reason at all to suspect that the fate of the twentieth-century USA would be any different. All the signs were there in escalating military spending and the massive growth in US debt, which made the approaching cataclysm seem just around the corner. However, it was also clear that the Kennedy thesis of 'over-extension' had a series of political allies amongst opponents of Ronald Reagan's economic and diplomatic policy. The fear of 'over-extension' was an especially useful card to play against an administration that seemed hell-bent on hiking defence expenditure at the expense of developing the rest of the domestic economy.

However, the geopolitical seismic shock that occurred the following year did not bring the collapse of the US economy and military machine, but instead irrevocably altered the map of Eastern Europe. The collapse of the Berlin Wall, and the domino-like collapse of the states of the former Eastern Bloc, suggested to casual observers that Kennedy's idea of 'over-extension' was somehow mistaken. He had gone into some considerable detail to discuss the warning signs of 'over-extension' – indeed the detail and plausibility of what he had been suggesting had been compelling enough for it to be taken seriously on Capitol Hill. Yet it was perhaps forgotten that Kennedy had been speculating in his attempt to draw lessons for the future from what the history of the past had been telling him. Whilst historians had disagreed with aspects of the history he had written, others were starting to queue up to attack his predictions.

Those who were relieved that it was the Soviet Bloc that had in fact collapsed were the first to pour scorn on Kennedy's apparently false predictions of doom for the USA. Kennedy's predictions of decline had been wrong about America and it was these that hit the headlines in the rush to discredit his ideas. What many conveniently forgot was that he had been right about the general idea of decline and that he had in fact predicted the growing weakness of Russian power in the Eastern Bloc. Moreover it was scarcely the whole book that had been discredited. The work investigating the Habsburg and British empires had not been in vain and remained good history. In the end, both empires could still be shown to have been victims of the 'over-extension' thesis. It seemed that Kennedy's error had been to make predictions at all! Some historians were privately of the opinion that Paul Kennedy had been rash to speculate about the future and suggested that this was trap that could ensnare any historian. This was the natural consequence for anyone who stepped out of the comfort zone of the past and spoke about the future.

However, even Kennedy's historical interpretation of the past came into question, as his theories were critically scrutinized by individuals outside the discipline of history. Henry Nau wrote a persuasive evaluation of the book in an article assessing its value some years later. This was published in the *Review of International Studies* which ostensibly served the scholarly worlds of politics and international relations. This article pulled no punches and began with the audacious title 'Why "The Rise and Fall of the Great Powers" was wrong'. Nau argued that many of the crucial aspects of Kennedy's general theory of 'over-extension' were substantially false and actually began to unpick the historical nature of some of Kennedy's assertions and writing. Nau very much had the benefit of hindsight, since he was writing in 2000 which gave over ten years' perspective on the predictions that had so concerned everybody a decade earlier. This meant that his challenge to Kennedy's history and its logic also contained criticism of Kennedy's predictions for the future, precisely because these relied on Kennedy's reading of history being correct. Thus elements of his historical model were being challenged, as was the value of this model in explaining past historical instances *or* the future.

Firstly he suggested that Kennedy's emphasis on the factors that were external to the countries he described rather overlooked many of the changes that were occurring inside these countries. Nau argued that these were every bit as important as the great power struggles Kennedy described. *The Rise and Fall of the Great Powers*, so Nau argued, had neglected the realm of domestic politics and its power to shape policies which preserved states that would otherwise slide into decline. This was what Nau suggested had happened to the USA, which had substantially saved itself from budget deficit in the years immediately following the publication of Kennedy's book. Indeed it was America's thoroughly unexpected ability to turn its situation around that seemed quite damning to Kennedy's 'over-extension thesis'. America's very maintenance of its defence spending had bankrupted the Soviet Bloc, allowing the country thereafter to rein in its own defence budget and thus prevent 'overstretch'.

Nau also suggested that Kennedy's desire to make his theory work had also described nations since 1500 as essentially the same, with similar responses to the perceived strength or weakness of their neighbours or rivals. It was also noted in this critical appraisal of *Rise* that there were a significant number of factors, during the twentieth century, that made nations converge as much as oppose one another in armed camps. The rise of fully mature and functioning democratic systems towards the end of the nineteenth century was a significant element in ending the quest for superiority. Nau noted that 'the democratic countries almost never fight each other', with this assertion vindicated by the makeup of the opposing sides through two World Wars and the Cold War beyond this. Once again the focus on external politics in Kennedy's argument missed some of the things that inspired the actions of nation states since his starting date of 1500. The early Reformation period was focused very much on religion and religious confession as the ideology most likely to inform friendship and alliance as much as economic battle and struggle. Nau asserted that Europe divided along confessional lines and not the economic and military power blocs Kennedy had suggested. The motivating factors did change over time with cultural factors replacing religion, whilst these were themselves replaced by the nineteenth-century obsession with nationalism and national identity. Finally the twentieth century had seen the issue of ideology predominate in the relations between states.

In addition, Nau argued that the period had also witnessed the power of technology as an increasingly important element in the equation. In the earlier phase of his writings Kennedy had noted that some technological breakthroughs were essential to his story of national/imperial struggle and 'over-extension'. Advances in gun and cannon design, naval shipbuilding, and military practice all, at one stage or another, gave some nations significant advantages over others – making struggles and battles more likely. However, Nau pointed out that the actual contemporary history of the period Kennedy had been speculating about ten years previously did not really bear this out.

The arrival of strategic and tactical nuclear weapons produced not enhanced struggle but actually a form of stable stalemate whereby war was avoided and conflict, such as it was, occurred through other means. Whilst technological advances may have happened, they were not responsible for seismic changes and shifts in the balance of power between great powers. The final collapse of the old Soviet Bloc was, in the end, caused by an expensive arms race rather than an actual conflict. Perhaps more important still, technology was also responsible for a revolution in communications which brought the world closer together at the same time as it made it more homogeneous. What became globalization also transformed markets and economic systems so rapidly during the 1990s that the future world sketched by Kennedy appeared a distant memory by 2005.

A worldwide culture seemed to be producing a so-called 'global village', where sharing and exchanging were more important than disagreement and conflict. Indeed this had persuaded another historian, Francis Fukuyama, to suggest that the world was so stable under capitalist social democratic systems that we could consider that history had 'come to an end'. However, this stability and peace was not of course universal, since trouble spots in places like the Middle East, Central America, and parts of Africa still defied this idea. Nonetheless the new phenomenon of the 'global village' was a far cry from the realpolitik world of conflict that Paul Kennedy had suggested.

If Henry Nau had merely been trying to point out the shortcomings of Kennedy's idea of 'over-extension', then this would have been a valuable contribution to assisting our understanding of a very difficult theory. However, Nau was unable to resist the chance to play the game too. He had begun the piece by showing why Kennedy's 'predictions' had not, to his mind, come to fruition. Nonetheless Nau chose to ignore the perils of speculating about what is to come. He wrote:

It is possible that the American and European renaissance is a temporary blip and that Japan and other Asian nations are poised to resume their meteoric rise. Russia and China too may just need more time to adapt to a rapidly globalizing world economy. Nevertheless, the deviations after almost fifteen years in directions opposite to those Kennedy predicted are not trivial. Kennedy did not expect them, and these directions do not seem likely to be reversed quickly. It is just as possible that the United States and now Europe will pull further ahead in the new information economy, that Russia and China will fall farther behind, and that Japan will remain in the position of a catch-up country rather than the leading economic power that Kennedy (and others) foresaw.

And again at the end of the piece:

> The perspective offered in this critique of Paul Kennedy's best-selling book paints a very different picture of the world at the beginning of the twenty-first century. In the domestic struggle to liberate individual initiative and create competitive markets, the countries of the Pacific region face significant handicaps. Their collectivist and Statist traditions do not fit well with the entrepreneurial requirements of the information age.

Obviously the years since Nau wrote his own critique of Kennedy have allowed some of his predictions to fall out of favour and lose relevance. We might consider that Nau has perhaps been too optimistic in his suggestion that Europe might once again be a realistically heavyweight power bloc and it is striking just how outdated his description of China looks from the perspective of today. Not simply has the West, and Western companies, been forthright in exporting manufacturing tools, plant, and technology to China, but the comparative advantage the latter has in labour costs makes this an almost inevitable one-way process. Other countries on the Pacific Rim, such as Vietnam, Indonesia, and the Philippines, have led a quiet economic revolution as their own low labour costs now successfully compete with China's. China's ability to forgo consumption whilst the West immerses itself in a credit-driven bubble has meant that China is now the creditor of significant portions of the West's debt. Perhaps this will lead inevitably to China's dominance as the central and pre-eminent world power in the first half of the twenty-first century. Alternatively China might well be only a part of an economic system in which a whole host of areas that were previously underdeveloped in the twentieth century reach dominance. These BRIC economies (Brazil, Russia, India, and China) may be the empires of the future yet to be rivalled and, who knows, supplanted by the growing power of the MINT (Mexico, Indonesia, Nigeria, and Turkey) economies.

The eagle-eyed reader, especially one who picks this book up in five, ten, or fifty years' time, will have noticed that at the end of the last paragraph I have made a prediction built on the suggestions of Henry Nau, built on the suggestions of Paul Kennedy. One, any, or all of us could be entirely wrong in our predictions, or if we are lucky we might be right with one or two of them. However (with the exception of my own prediction, which was wilful), they demonstrate how easy it is to play the game of predicting the future from the past. This, as Kennedy noted, was also useful in looking backwards at the history he had sketched since 1500. The present and possibly the future, for him, made the past more explicable and capable of analysis. In a sense this reminds us that one tool historians use to envisage how an event occurred in the past is to draw on their own experience of life within their own time. If we want to know how people reacted in the past, we sometimes have to put ourselves in their shoes. This creates a dialogue between the past and the present. Our known facts about the past blend with our knowledge of the current world – together they produce an analysis of how the past must have been. They also create the capacity for historians to use the past to look tentatively at the future.

Kennedy, Nau, and I are not at fault for trying to use history to explain the future, as long as the pitfalls and problems associated with doing this are kept in mind. This is especially important since none of us are entirely in control of how these speculations work out, or how people themselves will use such predictions. Kennedy was not simply at the mercy of history, or even of his critics, but he was profoundly at the mercy of public expectation. His ideas had been taken up and taken seriously by those who were scared and, importantly, by those who politically liked the sound of his explanation. Whilst history and the theories it generates are not infallible guides to the future, it is a far safer bet that a deep understanding of the past will enable us to understand the future. Much more importantly, it will give us examples from the past 'to think with' when we encounter and have to adapt to changing circumstances.

Indeed this has been important in one of Kennedy's later works, *Engineers of Victory*, published in 2013. In this he outlined how many fundamental obstacles faced by those fighting the Second World War (submarine warfare in the Atlantic, escorting bombers over heavily defended German cities, taking the war across vast distances to engage with the Japanese) were solved by what he termed 'tweakers' or problem solvers. Readily Kennedy himself realized the potential appeal of his work to the contemporary world when, towards the end of the book, he cited Apple's Steve Jobs as one of the most effective 'tweakers' of other people's half-ideas and crude experimental prototypes. As Kennedy himself stated, 'By extension, then, a smart middle manager or management consultant in today's business world – or a CEO who reads widely – can see the lessons that emerge from these tales'. Once again the tantalizing possibilities inherent in historical examples were becoming potential food for thought amongst a new generation seeking to solve everyday problems.

Historical explanations of what happened in the past are often based on theories. These are based on evidence and are a component of the narrative a historian tells about the past. They also provide an important tool for any historian analysing subsequent versions of the same occurrence. Thus knowing about theories and how they work, alongside what they explain (and perhaps do not explain), is important for placing history in patterns. Thus being aware of the work of others, and knowing and being able to understand and apply theories, are essential items in the toolbox of all historians.

7

Bringing it all together – the history of witchcraft

This chapter demonstrates many, or most, of the themes and aspects covered in the earlier sections, and makes an attempt to pull them all together. This revisits concepts that should now be familiar and makes clear the value, and sometimes pitfalls, of what is used to create and write history. This allows a further encounter with issues around causality and the search for truth, theory and its benefits/dangers, and the discovery of new historical sources and critical engagement with them. This also touches on issues of heritage and memory, the history of mentalities, and the impact of academic disciplines other than history. Ultimately this chapter enables us to show how they all blend into a wide and deep explanation of historical phenomena in the remote past.

Clearly the best way to see all of this action is to follow a worked example of intense and sometimes speculative historical debate. Ideally we need a self-contained episode, sufficiently far in the historical past for us to gain a decent historical perspective. It also needs to have generated significant levels of academic writing and controversy, as well as have a developed level of appeal to the history-reading and documentary-watching public. Luckily we have such episodes in abundance and one of the best examples is the history of witchcraft in early modern Europe. This is because it is a largely self-contained episode that includes forms of attitude and behaviour that appear sufficiently remote from our time to require historical explanation. In our study we will focus on the theories of historians about why and how Europe prosecuted and executed women and men as witches between 1450 and 1750.

Strangely historians were quite slow in recognizing the important and interesting perspectives that could be found from examining the history of witchcraft; sustained modern interest really only stems from the latter part of the twentieth century. Certainly historians were aware of the bare facts. Western Europe began to search for and prosecute women (and some men) for the crime of witchcraft from approximately 1450 onwards. These prosecutions tended to go in waves and often concentrated themselves around local areas and regions, where they would then die down only to be revived at a future date. Historians were dimly aware that witch-hunting was more likely to occur in some areas (Germany, France, Spain, and Italy) and less likely to appear in others (England, Scotland, and the American colonies). They were also reasonably certain that they could date the end of witch-hunting as a meaningful phenomenon to roughly the middle of the eighteenth century, where thereafter it appeared to die out somewhat rapidly. For some this was a convenient way to say that the modern world had arrived, where explanations for what mankind observed were governed by more rational and scientific reasoning.

Historians thus discovered that the ground-breaking work in witchcraft studies was being done by other disciplines. Chief amongst these were anthropologists working in the early years of the twentieth century, who took their inspiration from studying contemporary societies in far-flung corners of the world. Such practitioners were constantly comparing cultures and identifying aspects that were common or different. Inevitably some of what they found made them think deeply about the past of European cultures and the societies that bred them.

Perhaps the first of these that made a truly significant impact was Sir James Frazer, who wrote a highly influential book entitled *The Golden Bough* which appeared in 1890. This was a part of early anthropology's ambitious mission to explain all cultures and to look for similar cultural archetypes throughout the world. These, so Frazer argued, were aspects common to primitive cultures no matter where they were located. Frazer's main proposition was that he could show that there had been an almost worldwide belief in the idea of a sacred king who had been sacrificed. This essential story could be found to be common to cultures on every continent. So *The Golden Bough* saw itself as a primer for those seeking to think about comparative anthropology. Whilst this book did not expressly talk about witchcraft, and is now viewed as somewhat old-fashioned by contemporary anthropologists, there were those who were greatly taken with Frazer's basic ideas. His search for archetypes seemed plausible and many sought to apply this principle to the study of witchcraft and its past in Europe.

The most important of these was another anthropologist, Margaret Murray, who initially became interested in fertility and cults and wrote a history of them in the years immediately after the First World War. But it rapidly became clear that she had an ambition to follow in the universalizing footsteps of Frazer. This search for common cultural roots amongst us all was also a specific product of the years after the First World War, which had seen the differences between peoples degenerate into carnage and destruction. This indicates again to us the importance of context, and how this influences the direction of historical study. Margaret Murray was also determined to undermine male dominance in conventional religion. This also fitted with a number of early twentieth-century religious movements, such as Theosophy, which had made a point of emphasizing the innate and privileged spirituality of women, which its advocates believed had been neglected up to this point. These tributaries of thought led Murray into some specific directions. She argued that what historians had identified as the 'witch cult' was universal throughout Europe. She suggested that her research had uncovered that it was a simple and ancient fertility cult that had been stamped out by the aggression of conventional Christian individuals and institutions. She also suggested that these fertility cults were substantially harmless and that their presence in Europe pre-dated Christianity. In this respect she was the forerunner of some feminist arguments that saw witch-hunting as a method by which male-dominated patriarchal structures were seeking to discipline women and rob them of all power. But Murray went further to argue that she could be certain, from the evidence she had uncovered, that all witch covens had exactly thirteen members. She also believed that witches had actually taken part in the activities to which they subsequently confessed. Thus Murray concluded that the actions and activities were real and that these had been distorted and misrepresented by subsequent historical sources. This was important because some nineteenth-century thinkers, basking in rationality and reason, had readily concluded that the primitive nature of early modern Christianity had unjustly and callously made innocent victims of many in the name of fear and misunderstanding.

But as the study of witchcraft began to gather pace in the twentieth century, many began to notice a great many problems with the world of witches as sketched by Margaret Murray. Her covens of exactly thirteen witches were designed to show off the uniformity of the belief system throughout Europe, but some noticed that the evidence was simply not universal. Indeed several suggested that she had actively been selective with her evidence and even manipulated some of it to produce examples that validated her theories. She was also accused of taking the evidence offered by so-called witches in court far too readily at face value. Those who confessed could have been frightened of authority, the victims of judicial torture, seeking to implicate others as a result of local neighbourhood disputes, or the victims of mental instability. Murray categorically refused to consider any of these possibilities and instead resolutely insisted that all who gave evidence about their own witchcraft acts, or those of others, were telling the truth. But, importantly, we should note that she possibly had no choice but to do so for her ideas to remain coherent – particularly since we can suspect she was so determined that witchcraft should exist as a viable alternative religion to Christianity. Murray passionately believed in her ideas and eventually took the logical step of offering support to the late twentieth-century Wiccan movement; perhaps here indicating a moment when the historian can eventually be led to become an activist by the consequences of their own thought.

Murray also suggested that the so-called 'witches' sabbat' (where her covens of thirteen met to worship their fertility god, conveniently turned into the devil by hostile Christianity) was universal. Yet it was already apparent that the 'witches' sabbat' was very obviously missing from England where maleficium (or doing evil acts towards one's neighbours without invoking the devil) was, almost exclusively, the only offence associated with witchcraft. One historian who took the lead in criticizing Murray was Norman Cohn who, in his 1975 book *Europe's Inner Demons*, ran a fine-toothed comb over her scholarship and its implications for the study of witchcraft. He established that she had, in other areas, been less than truthful. Norman Cohn followed her trail back into the documents to look at the sources she had used and his discoveries were quite surprising. Murray had read and quoted selectively, looking at passages where ritual low-level magic had been portrayed and choosing to quote only these. Cohn could show conclusively that Murray had decided to neglect the parts where people claimed they flew to coven meetings or changed into animals, because this clearly conflicted with her theory about taking witches seriously all of the time. It was now quite obvious that Murray had constructed her model of witchcraft and then hammered the evidence to fit. In particular Cohn attacked Murray's assertion that witches had been persecuted simple pagans, undone by their contact with the aggressor religion – Christianity. He concluded:

> The picture of the sabbat which took shape in the first decades of the fifteenth century was a modern elaboration, by lay and ecclesiastical judges and demonologists, of an aggressive stereotype that had been applied in former times to Jews, the early Christians, and medieval heretical sects.

Cohn himself also had his own contribution to make to the historiography of witchcraft studies. He demonstrated, quite convincingly, that some early witchcraft documents on which great reliance had been placed were actually later forgeries intended to mislead. This led him to consider that moral panics, or scapegoating, had clearly occurred throughout the medieval and early modern period. Fear had led individuals and populations to lose their sense of proportion and thus to accuse their friends, neighbours, and families of all sorts of unspeakable crimes against them, through the use of ritual magic. So he looked for what he called Europe's 'inner demons'; the collective psychological stress caused by social and economic change that led people to fantasize about evil and malevolence. For Cohn this was the secret of and the explanation for early modern Europe's obsession with hunting down the witches in its midst.

Later historians would not entirely forsake the value of anthropological approaches; despite the fact Margaret Murray had given them a bad name. The historian Alan Macfarlane was the first (in 1970) to write properly in depth about the history of witchcraft in England, and he was well schooled in the discipline of anthropology as much as he was an able historian. Macfarlane wrote about the English county of Essex – the county with by far the greatest level of witchcraft activity in England. He found that witches and their accusers were from significantly different social backgrounds. Those who accused individuals of witchcraft were predominantly of higher social status than those who found themselves accused. This offered him a somewhat different perspective on what was happening in early modern England.

This set Macfarlane thinking that there might be underlying social reasons why witchcraft accusations occurred. Ultimately, his study of witchcraft in Essex concluded that social attitudes to charity and almsgiving had significantly altered during this period. He saw the Reformation's destruction of the monasteries and their communal approaches to welfare as important in this process. At a time when crop yields were falling and it was becoming more difficult to make ends meet, more individuals were forced to the very margins of survival. In this much more unstable society, more and more people went from house to house begging or seeking unofficial welfare from others. Macfarlane argued this meant that more people in a socially superior position began to resent this. Yet they still felt guilty for their refusal to offer even temporary charity to those falling on hard times. As Macfarlane argued, this society had become precarious, with the slightest ailment afflicting crops or livestock capable of tipping the balance against individuals. If you were faced with such guilt or misfortune then you might well seek to 'blame' someone for this. Macfarlane argued this was how the witch-hunts in Essex arose.

But Macfarlane had an agenda beyond the simple history of witchcraft. He liked anthropology, but he liked the discipline of sociology as well and was ultimately a devotee of modernization theory. Basically this starts its exploration of history firmly from the present and looks back for signposts to show how the world we live in today came about through definitive moments of improvement. Looking back from the England of the late 1970s and early 1980s, Macfarlane saw the witches of Essex fitting into a wider pattern. Thus the witches of Essex were unfortunate victims of the growing English entrepreneurial spirit, a cultural idea fostered by conservative agendas in the 1980s in particular. Economic change had marginalized the victims of witchcraft accusations. However, Macfarlane, through his history, was saying that they should have adapted, and it was just simply unfortunate they were the victims of a society that had dispensed with the desire, and even the need, to look after them.

Another historian to have put a unique stamp on the study of witchcraft, and to more than shake it up, was a historian we met in an earlier chapter concerning memory and mentalities – Carlo Ginzburg. When he uncovered the raw material for *The Cheese and the Worms* he was also working on a study of the phenomenon of witchcraft in the remote areas of north-eastern Italy. In the papal archives Ginzburg unearthed a grouping called the Benandanti who were located in the remote region of Friuli from which the miller, Menocchio, in *The Cheese and the Worms* had also come. Being a border region there were collisions of Italian, Germanic, and Balkan culture and folklore, demonstrating the potential universality of such stories. The Benandanti that Ginzburg had found were accused of witchcraft and a pact with the devil. They replied that they were no such thing and were in fact witch fighters rather than actual witches. They claimed that, along with real witches, they had out-of-body experiences four times a year (the so-called 'ember days' which coincided with the equinoxes). These experiences, or trances, enabled them to ride on the backs of wild animals to go and fight the real witches who threatened to destroy the coming year's crops. But, pushed into the mould of witch prosecution by the interrogation perpetrated by the Inquisition, eventually under torture one confessed to being a witch and then implicated others to produce, sadly, a stereotypical witch-hunt.

Although this said much about the Inquisition stereotyping people, it also said something more deeply disturbing for the historiography of witchcraft. If Ginzburg was correct then historians might have to face the fact that Margaret Murray's work on fertility cults may actually have had some credibility, in spite of her selective reading of the evidence, her falsification of facts, and her blind assertions from little evidence. The Benandanti did not meet in thirteens, but they were a fertility cult she would have recognized, with apparently benign motives far removed from the devil-worshipping threat to the divine order that the Inquisition thought they were.

Ginzburg's conclusions were very firmly echoed by his later work which appeared in his subsequent book *Ecstasies*, which concentrated firmly on the 'witches' sabbat' as a pan-European phenomenon. In this work Ginzburg concluded:

> In the image of the Sabbath we distinguished two cultural currents, of diverse origin: on the one hand, as elaborated by inquisitors and lay judges, the theme of a conspiracy plotted by a sect or hostile group; on the other, elements of shamanistic origin which were now rooted in folk culture, such as the magic flight and animal metamorphosis. But this juxtaposition is too schematic. The moment has come to acknowledge the fact that the fusion between the two lodes could only have been so firm and enduring in so far as there existed a substantial subterranean affinity between them. The witches' sabbat is the place where myths and their uses merge like tributaries into a river.

Ginzburg's conclusions here arguably reached back beyond Margaret Murray to echo Sir James Frazer and the conclusions of the earlier anthropologists about the essentially enduring nature of fertility cults.

Yet other historians, such as Robin Briggs (writing in 1998), looked elsewhere to see witchcraft as a function of neighbourhood disputes. On the basis of Alan Macfarlane's assumptions about the precariousness of economic existence, this theory focused on how this issue fed neighbourhood disputes. In many European countries individuals, communities, and families took up these disputes and fused them under pressure into witchcraft accusations. This could draw upon disputes over land, family feuds, or long-held grievances, sometimes stretching back over many generations. This was seen as one of the possible explanations for the famous Salem witch-hunts (in Massachusetts, USA). Two historians, Paul Boyer and Stephen Nissenbaum, in the book *Salem Possessed*, in 1974, did significant family reconstruction work to be able to suggest that a pattern emerged in the 1692 witch-hunt in Salem. The accused could be traced back to one family with growing mercantile interests and the accusers traced back to another supporting the more traditional agricultural lifestyle. These families had quarrelled acrimoniously for some years before the witchcraft accusations. Briggs, Boyer and Nissenbaum, and others represent a school of thought that has been convinced that the witch-hunts were a species of scapegoating and escalating quarrels, where conflicting interests harshly pitched individuals against one another. For these theorists this really indicated the squeeze put upon subsistence living during the early modern period. This had resulted in people blaming each other for the dangerous and threatening misfortunes that befell them.

Other historians have looked closely at the law, seeing this as responsible for prolonging and exacerbating witch-hunts throughout Europe. In particular many historians have seen the evolution of the law as central to the direction and pattern of early modern witch-hunting – some go as far as to say it was a precondition for it. Ostensibly, it was the law which formulated the crimes and charged individuals with maleficium and/or complicity in the 'witches' sabbat'. This was happening at a time when conceptions of the law, its possibility and purpose were in a state of considerable flux. Some historians noted that England appeared to be comparatively free from witch-hunts during the early modern period. Whilst vast outbreaks of witch-hunting occurred in Germany and central Europe, England experienced only isolated and small incidents, which made for a vastly different pattern of witchcraft and its detection. One reason offered for this was the significant difference in the law and how its basic principles operated in these different countries. In most of Europe there was a pronounced shift away from 'accusatorial' justice towards 'inquisitorial' justice, as a result of the revived study of Roman law which commenced in the twelfth century.

The accusatorial system relied on individuals to bring prosecutions against their neighbours. These were generally brought to local courts and local systems of justice, and were held before judges and magistrates who were connected with the local community. Individuals who brought such charges then had to be prepared to affirm the truth of these in court, opposite the person they had accused. As we can all imagine, this was much more of a commitment for individuals to undertake. Accusing one of your neighbours of witchcraft was not to be done lightly, and these legal procedures must have dissuaded many from following this course of action. Generally speaking, by the end of the medieval period, the person accused of a crime in the accusatorial system would have to undergo trial by ordeal. That is, undertaking a hazardous task such as retrieving a stone from a cauldron of boiling water. This involved them putting their protested innocence in the hands of God who was believed to grant such miracles to the innocent. Contemporary knowledge of witchcraft also revived the trial by water or 'ducking' of a suspect witch. Alternatively suspects were allowed to collect individuals from within their local community who would be prepared to swear to their good character (so-called oath helpers). If these methods of seeking an acquittal were to prove successful, then the individual who had made the original accusation might consider they had damaged their own standing within the community. All such calculations probably deterred a great many from making accusations of witchcraft against their neighbours.

This accusatorial system was very much based on local answers to local problems within the community. Historians of the law see this as indicative of pre-modern law and pre-modern states – the process of modernization is the process of the state starting to become interested in this area of law. The state interest in policing and regulating communities led to the rise of the 'inquisitorial' system. As the name implies, this empowered judges to enquire into the crime. Such judges frequently arrived in, or effectively 'parachuted' into, communities from the outside, bringing other interests and agendas. To enquire into crimes like witchcraft, they had the power to call witnesses or indeed any individual who might enable them to determine beyond doubt the truth of any matter. To ensure they gained as much valuable information as possible, these hearings occurred in private and away from the courtroom where they were carefully recorded and annotated by an army of secretaries and scribes.

The leading impetus behind the 'inquisitorial' system came from the papacy when, in the early years of the thirteenth century, Pope Gregory IX moved to establish an organization with sole responsibility for seeking and destroying heresy. Although it was to become renowned for its persuasive methods of eliciting confessions from victims, it is often forgotten that the most powerful tool at its disposal was its ability to collect and store information about the people it had questioned. For the first time the production, collation, and storage of information became an activity in itself. It became possible to track the accused, their families, friends, and associates, across years, regions, and countries. This suggests another history playing itself out here – the history of the early modern state and its bureaucratic apparatus growing in sophistication and ambition, and this was to have implications for other subjects of historical enquiry. But the Inquisition was not the sole custodian of inquisitorial practice – prince bishops in Germany also used this method, as did several French parliaments held away from Paris. There was even a version of this in Scotland, where witch trials were centrally endorsed and sanctioned, but conducted on local terms and conditions.

The inquisitorial system allowed witchcraft prosecutions to flourish because it was some distance from central control and its regularized procedures. In the absence of this, inquisitors had considerable autonomy of action, and there is frequent evidence that inquisitors could do what they liked. When this was combined with the absence of disincentives present in the accusatorial system, the likelihood of witch trials increased considerably. Witchcraft became a *crimen exceptum* – essentially an exceptional crime. This term reveals the popular fear that the worldly methods of judges and courts and ecclesiastics were limited against the powers of darkness, persuading them to cast many of the conventional, accepted, and humane rules aside. For the first time officers of the court could initiate prosecutions – thus granting the pursuit of people a legal life of its own. What appeared to make this run spectacularly out of control, so some historians have noted, was that this process sanctioned the use of torture for the first time. Although the use of torture was more controlled and regulated than many people think, it still had inevitable results. The individual was encouraged to implicate others whilst under torture, and likewise they were persuaded to answer leading questions in a particular way. Very often the victim would give the inquisitor the answers they felt he wanted – generally confirming and enhancing stereotypes of the witch. Thus to some historians these changes, an almost total reconstruction of the law, were primarily responsible for the strength and dangerous exuberance of early modern European witch-hunting.

Sometimes in specific instances it is possible to see witch-hunts and outbreaks of witch-hunting orchestrated by the action of single individuals who became self-appointed witch-hunters. This largely explains the outbreak of witch-hunting in Essex in the late 1640s. This occurred during the height of the

English Civil War, which has led other historians to note how political vacuums tend to produce witch-hunting episodes. This phenomenon has been noted in England as well as in Germany during the Thirty Years' War.

Some other historians have taken a substantially different approach and have noted how much contemporary literature exists around witchcraft, going as far as to suggest that it was, perhaps, a preoccupation of the early modern period's learned and chattering classes. The search for witches and witchcraft emerges from this as a growing and fashionable pre-occupation of the intellectual elite. To back this theory up, historians tend to concentrate on Scotland as a prime example of this occurrence. Up until the 1590s Scotland was almost entirely devoid of witchcraft prosecutions. Meanwhile the country's monarch – king James VI of Scotland (eventually to become James I of England) – had been in Denmark to bring his bride (Anne of Denmark) back to Scotland. Whilst in Denmark the king had spent a great deal of time talking with the country's theologians and inevitably the conversation turned to evil, the devil, and the phenomenon of witches. James became convinced of the reality of witches, the threat they posed to the godly commonwealth, and to God's princes on earth. Such fears and suspicions were merely confirmed for him when he returned to Scotland, only for his small fleet of ships to be blown off course by a violent storm. In James's mind this could only have been caused by the diabolical intervention of a witch's coven and one was duly discovered at North Berwick. These 'witches' were imprisoned, tortured, and examined by James I himself. Their plot against him was supposedly verified by the fact that one witch, Agnes Sampson, was able to confirm to James the words he had spoken to his wife on their wedding night. Irrespective of whether this was true or not, there is certainly a case for arguing that Scotland had been free of witchcraft accusations and witch-hunts until the imagination of the monarch had been dramatically caught by the idea.

The history of witchcraft has also seen historians of gender note how witchcraft accusations seemed to be part of a much wider and longer gender war, asking, not unreasonably, 'Was witch-hunting woman-hunting?' Many historians noticed several ways in which witch-hunts picked specifically on women for a possible variety of motives. Women in most areas were far more likely to be accused of witchcraft. This was possibly because they were more likely to be involved in neighbourly disputes. Here the history of mundane things contributes significantly to our understanding. Our typical picture of the witch at work indicates the presence of a cooking pot, or cauldron, and a broomstick. These were both symbols of female work within the domestic world which, for most of the time, carried the simple significance of women providing for their families and keeping house. However, they became invested with different meaning within a changed context which saw the cauldron as a means of enacting spells and creating potions, whilst the otherwise innocent broomstick became a mode of transport to the 'witches' sabbat'. Some historians suggested women's similar connection to childbirth and healing placed them in 'the wrong place at the wrong time' if misfortune befell anyone in the vicinity. Some other historians suggested that there was a more widespread male conspiracy amongst the medical profession designed to undermine the power of popular healers, in preparation for the advance of professional medicine. Others saw a more widespread male fear of women's growing power and public visibility that meant witch-hunting was an excuse for reasserting discipline. Certainly the infamous text of the 1480s, the *Malleus Maleficarum*, the so-called 'Hammer of Witches', contained long diatribes against the sinfulness of women. This has been seen by generations of gender historians as fuelling the inbuilt misogyny against women exhibited by the trials and giving it theological backing. If this work were to be consulted, its inbuilt bias against women, and deep-seated suspicion of their motives and actions, would lend considerable credence to this view. However, these gender arguments were not conclusive, since they did not explain some areas where accusations against male witches constituted a significant proportion of the total. They also did not so easily account for the numerous instances in which women accused other women, nor did they satisfactorily explain, on their own, the passing of witch-hunting. Whilst the *Malleus Maleficarum* may be a misogynist text, it is scarcely representative and its author has effectively been shown to be mentally unstable. But some historians, such as Diane Purkiss, have put a more 'positive' slant on this phenomenon to argue that witchcraft and the sabbat allowed women actively to take power for themselves against a world ruled and controlled by men.

Alternatively, some have suggested that the early modern witch-hunts can be analysed through explanations that emanate from medicine and medical science. This also points to how different disciplines now interact more readily than they might have done fifty years ago. One of these explanations sought to portray witches as female healers who were consciously eradicated by the male medical profession that indulged in a patriarchal conspiracy. More subtle arguments noted that the medical knowledge of doctors themselves may have been a source of witchcraft accusations. The early modern period has been noted as a time when medical knowledge was in a state of flux. The old Galenic methods of describing the human body and its ailments – the so-called system of humours – which had been passed down from ancient Greece, was no longer accepted as a satisfactory framework of explanations. Modern medicine would eventually evolve from this questioning, but this change was not to occur overnight. The interim period meant that only partially satisfactory explanations served to help physicians in their work. This meant that diseases and phenomena that an individual doctor could not explain could easily be labelled a 'witch disease' and a perpetrator in the local community might then be sought out.

Another medical explanation for the witch-hunts has centred on early modern Europe's consumption of rye bread as a possible source of ergot poisoning. Scientists, drawing on evidence from some twentieth-century incidents, have cited the presence of the ergot fungus on rye bread as the potential cause of illnesses that would spawn witchcraft accusations. Ergot is chemically almost identical to lysergic acid (LSD) and it has been known to cause hallucinations and extreme physical convulsions. Biochemists, climatologists, social anthropologists, and historians have worked alongside one another and have suggested that ergot poisoning was responsible for some European witch-hunting outbreaks. In particular the work of Linnda Caporael has suggested ergot poisoning may have been especially responsible for the outbreak at Salem, Massachusetts, in 1692. Studying the location of rye crops, and examining what can be known of weather patterns in the areas concerned, historians such as Mary Matossian have noted the prevalence of the crop and the damp weather conditions that encouraged the growth of ergot. Descriptions of the convulsions and frantic behaviour of the victims are seen to mirror those of ergot poisoning. Thus, those who were victims of witchcraft may have been the victims of a collective form of poisoning which the community could not otherwise explain.

This chapter has discussed an important historical phenomenon explained in various ways by a number of historians. Such explanations have incorporated folk beliefs and mythology, anthropology and social structure, the history of ideas amongst elites, the impact of changes in the law, gender issues, and the history of medicine and health. Reading from the outside, it is possible to see any one of these explanations as more plausible than the others, or indeed to focus on a combination of these. We have seen how some theories can explain the pattern of historical events, but equally we have learned to spot the limitations of others. There has also been an investigation of the type of thinker and writer that history inspires to become historians. They are as different as history itself and appreciating this variety is also important in discovering how taste, and sometimes fashion, governs the history that the reader is likely to become interested in and seek to follow.

Likewise this chapter has also seen a number of the various tools at the disposal of the active historian applied to one area of historical investigation. We have looked at causes and the fact that their details must be placed chronologically, and in a credible order, if they are to retain their explanatory power. Likewise we have also seen in the approach of Margaret Murray both the importance of ascertaining the validity and truthfulness of a source and the problems for explanation when these can no longer be relied on. However, we also saw, in relation to her work, how the uncovering of new evidence may bring an older, discredited analysis back into fashion. The example of Margaret Murray also shows us how a historian is the product of their own times and may be persuaded to follow their own prejudices even into the contemporary world. The role of other disciplines informing history in the creation of theories has also been a factor evident in this study of witchcraft, with anthropology, medicine, biochemistry, legal studies, and psychology all having a role in providing material for possible explanations of the witch-hunt.

The whole history of witch-hunting also provides material for considering the role of memory in history. For contemporaries, memory functioned as a method of storing up knowledge about a woman, or women from the same family, that might eventually be used against them. This could form part of the collective memory of a community which could suddenly take action against an individual. The failure of witch and folk beliefs simply to die out in the eighteenth century also suggests that they retained power as memories and were sometimes called to mind when they were of value to people. The history of what happened to a specific group of women has been a formative experience for gender historians who wanted to provide explanations not just for this instance of oppression, but for the oppression of women in other historical situations. We might also think of how the memory bequeathed to us from the early modern period has been filtered through myth, misunderstanding, and the preconceptions and preoccupations of our own times to provide a series of memories unrelated to the reality of witchcraft's history. Shakespeare's *Macbeth* may have been nearer in time to the actual witch-hunts, but even this depiction contained its share of supposition and myth that has coloured how we think of witches. This in itself has a history and it will be the work of subsequent historians of our culture to assess how phenomena such as the *Harry Potter* canon of books and films have shaped the twenty-first century's attitude to witchcraft, magic, and the supernatural.

We have seen the essential building blocks of causality, theory, engagement with other disciplines, and the continual evaluation of evidence and research questions that makes up the daily task of the historian at large in the vast, and continually enthralling, field of history. This book has tried to introduce the importance of these fundamental tools to allow the reader to indulge in their own speculation about the history that interests them. This has avoided a simple catalogue of what other historians have said (plenty of these exist elsewhere), so that the enthusiastic reader and budding historian can be inspired to pursue their own path of exploration and investigation, with the aims of providing analysis and explanation. Hopefully, from here, the reader can set forth into the adventurous and constantly surprising landscape of history with a more confident outlook. Although the terrain can be difficult and rocky, this book can constitute a rudimentary compass which indicates the general direction in which to travel forward.

8
Conclusion

The book that you have just read by no means claims to tell the whole story about historical enquiry, although it offers a good and reassuring start. Hopefully it has explored some incidents and stories from history, whilst managing to investigate some of the preoccupations of the historian and the techniques that he or she uses. As we are now aware, historians must find evidence, evaluate the value and worth of that evidence, and then think what to do with it. They can use this to create explanations of historical happenings. As such they might find that explanation gets created from bias, the preoccupations of the historian's own age, and/or the ideological mindset of the historian themselves. However the historian chooses to do this, they will create a hierarchy of explanation which ranges from the fanciful through to the likely and the credible. We have seen in this book how this can be done well, but also how this can be done badly. The moral of this particular part of the story is that history is a discipline and all those seeking to practise it should be attentive at all times. However, this scarcely means it is not possible to be imaginative – to be caught up by the spirit of the subject and the desire to recreate and revisit the past.

Hopefully we have also seen some sense of the variety of types of history that are written. As we now are aware, historians write about economics, politics, the history of past societies, and even the mindset of individuals in the past, alongside many other topics that the reader can now investigate for themselves. What this should indicate to those interested in history is that it is possible for any reader or individual interested in the subject to find their niche. It is also more than likely that some parts of history will inevitably be more interesting to the individual than others. A glimpse of this variety will also show that a wide range of techniques and methods are likewise used to investigate many branches of the subject.

Although some of these are quite sophisticated and some of their practitioners bring to bear years of experience in remote and dusty archives, the chance to be a practising historian is excitingly open to all of us. If there is one fundamentally important aspect of the subject the reader should take away from this volume it is that the vital task of the historian is to ask questions. In many respects this has essentially been the underlying theme of the book – to equip the reader to ask pertinent questions. It has shown how we should all learn to interrogate and question in an effective way, but also how historians have questions asked of them and how different evidence creates new questions. We have also learned how the answers this questioning brings forth can sometimes turn history upside down. We have even seen evidence of what happens when historians do not ask the right questions, or are prevented from asking them at all.

Thus your experience of thinking through the issues posed by this book should persuade you that you are equipped to ask questions about the history you encounter; whether this is looking at sources and primary material at first hand, or whether it is reading and thinking about the work produced by another historian. Asking questions about how what you are reading relates to what you know – what within it appears to be breaking new ground and speaking to the bigger picture – is a task the reader can now accomplish. In the bibliography are a few suggestions about taking the themes and issues contained in the chapters a little further and deeper. Some of the works cited also add perspectives and different slants on the specific history discussed in the respective chapters. Also mentioned are some other works that contain themes only partially related to the specifics of a particular chapter. These offer the chance to go off on a tangent that may prove interesting to many readers.

Bibliography and further reading

There are a bewildering number of books which claim to be viable and useful introductions to historical study. This guide can only mention a few of them that seem well placed to provide helpful insights.

General

Benjamin, J.R. 2010. *The Student's Guide to History*, 12th edn. New York, Palgrave Macmillan

Brown, C. 2005. *Postmodernism for Historians*. London, Pearson Longman

Budd, A., ed. 2009. *The Modern Historiography Reader*. Abingdon, Routledge

Roberts, G. 2001. *The History and Narrative Reader*. London, Routledge

Stanford, M. 1996. *A Companion to the Study of History*. Oxford, Blackwell

Thompson, W. 2004. *Postmodernism and History*. Basingstoke, Palgrave Macmillan

Tosh, J, ed. 2009. *Historians on History*, 2nd edn. London, Pearson Longman

Tosh, J. 2010. *The Pursuit of History*, 5th edn. London, Pearson Longman

Writing about history

Berger, S., Feldner, H., and Passmore, K, eds. 2010. *Writing History: Theory and Practice*. New York, Bloomsbury

Black, J., and MacRaild, D. 2007. *Studying History.* Basingstoke, Palgrave Macmillan

Marius, R., and Page, M.E. 1989. *A Short Guide to Writing about History.* New York, HarperCollins

Wifesale

Foucault, M. 1978. *The History of Sexuality Volume 1.* New York, Random House

Foucault, M. 1985. *The History of Sexuality Volume 2.* New York, Random House

Foucault, M. 1986. *The History of Sexuality Volume 3.* New York, Random House

Macfarlane, A. 1986. *Marriage and Love in England 1300–1840.* Oxford, Blackwell

Menefee, S.P. 1984. *Wives for Sale: an Ethnographic Study of Popular Divorce.* Oxford, Blackwell

Thompson, E.P. 1991. *Customs in Common.* London, Merlin Press

Hitler's diaries

Harris, R. 1986. *Selling Hitler.* London, Arrow

Queen Victoria and haemophilia

Potts, D.M., and Potts, W.T.W. *Queen Victoria's Gene: Haemophilia and the Royal Family.* Stroud, The History Press

Menocchio

Ginzburg, C. 1980. *The Cheese and the Worms.* Baltimore, Johns Hopkins University Press

If the reader gains a taste for this investigation of cultural history, through the 'episode a chapter' format, it is worth recommending two other works in the same mould:

Cressy, D. 2001. *Agnes Bowker's Cat: Travesties and Transgressions in Tudor and Stuart England*. Oxford, Oxford University Press

Darnton, R. 2009. *The Great Cat Massacre and Other Episodes in French Cultural History*. New York, Basic Books

The social history of death

Ariès, P. 1991. *The Hour of Our Death*. New York, Vintage

Dickens, A.G. 1964. *The English Reformation*. State College, Pennsylvania State University Press

War

Inglis, K. 2006. *Sacred Places: War Memorials in the Australian Landscape*. Melbourne, Melbourne University Press

Turner, F. 2001. *Echoes of Combat: Trauma, Memory and the Vietnam War*. Minneapolis, University of Minnesota Press

Winter, J. 1998. *Sites of Memory, Sites of Mourning: The Great War in European Cultural History*. Cambridge, Cambridge University Press

Winter, J., and Sivan, E., eds. 2008. *War and Remembrance in the Twentieth Century*. Cambridge, Cambridge University Press

The history of alcohol

Brandwood, G.K. 2004. *Licensed to Sell: The History and Heritage of the Public House*. Farnham, English Heritage

Clark, P. 1983. *The English Alehouse*. Harlow, Longman

Hobsbawm, E., and Ranger, T., eds. 1992. *The Invention of Tradition*. Cambridge, Cambridge University Press

Jennings, P. 2007. *The Local: A History of the English Pub*. Stroud, The History Press

For fascinating insights into the culture (and taste) of beer the reader is advised to consult the numerous works of Michael Jackson, the famously self-styled 'Beer Hunter'.

The abolition of slavery

James, C.L.R. 2001. *The Black Jacobins*. London, Penguin

Walvin, J. 1992. *Black Ivory: a History of British Slavery*. London, HarperCollins

Walvin, J. 1996. *Questioning Slavery*. London, Routledge

Walvin, J. 2007. *A Short History of Slavery*. London, Penguin

Walvin, J. 2007. *The Trader, the Owner, the Slave: Parallel Lives in the Age of Slavery*. London, Jonathan Cape

Williams, E. 1994. *Capitalism and Slavery*. Chapel Hill, University of North Carolina Press

Changing histories

Kennedy, P. 1987. *The Rise and Fall of the Great Powers: Economic Change and Military Conflict from 1500–2000*. New York, Vintage

Kennedy, P. 1981. *The Realities Behind Diplomacy: Background Influences on British External Policy 1865–1980*. London, George Allen and Unwin

Kennedy, P. 1992. *Strategy and Diplomacy 1870–1945*. London, HarperCollins

Kennedy, P., ed. 1992. *Grand Strategies in War and Peace*. New Haven, Yale University Press

Kennedy, P. 1994. *Preparing for the Twenty First Century*. New York, Vintage

Kennedy, P. 2004. *The Rise and Fall of British Naval Mastery*. London, Penguin

Kennedy, P. 2007. *The Parliament of Man: The Past Present and Future of the United Nations*. London, Penguin

Kennedy, P. 2013. *Engineers of Victory: The Problem Solvers who Turned the Tide in the Second World War.* London, Allen Lane

The history of witchcraft

Ankarloo, B., and Henningsen, G., eds. 1989. *Early Modern European Witchcraft: Centres and Peripheries.* Oxford, Oxford University Press

Caporael, L.R. 1976. 'Ergotism: The Satan Loosed in Salem?' *Science*, 192: 21–26

Clark, S. 1997. *Thinking with Demons: The Idea of Witchcraft in Early Modern Europe.* Oxford, Oxford University Press

Davies, O. 2004. *Beyond the Witch Trials: Witchcraft and Magic in Enlightenment Europe.* Manchester, Manchester University Press

Ginzburg, C. 1983. *The Night Battles: Witchcraft and Agrarian Cults in the Sixteenth and Seventeenth Centuries.* Baltimore, Johns Hopkins University Press

Goodare, J., ed. 2002. *The Scottish Witch-Hunt in Context.* Manchester, Manchester University Press

Larner, C. 1981. *Enemies of God: The Witch-Hunt in Scotland.* Baltimore, Johns Hopkins University Press

Levack, B. 2013. *The Oxford Handbook of Witchcraft in Early Modern Europe and Colonial America.* Oxford, Oxford University Press

Levack, B. 2013. *The Witch-hunt in Early Modern Europe*, 3rd edn. Abingdon, Routledge

Macfarlane, A. 1999. *Witchcraft in Tudor and Stuart England: A Regional and Comparative Study*, 2nd edn. London, Routledge

Matossian, M. K. 1991. *Poisons of the Past: Molds, Epidemics and History.* New Haven, Yale University Press

Purkiss, D. 1996. *The Witch in History: Early Modern and Twentieth-Century Representations.* London, Routledge

Sharpe, J.A. 1996. *Instruments of Darkness: Witchcraft in England 1550–1750.* London, Penguin

Sharpe, J.A. 1999. *The Bewitching of Anne Gunter: A Horrible and True Story of Football, Witchcraft, Murder and the King of England*. London, Profile Books

Thomas, K. 1991. *Religion and the Decline of Magic: Studies in Popular Beliefs in Sixteenth- and Seventeenth-Century England*. London, Penguin

The Salem witch-hunt of 1692

Boyer, P., and Nissenbaum, S., eds. 1974. *Salem Possessed: The Social Origin of Witchcraft*. Cambridge, MA, Harvard University Press

Boyer, P., and Nissenbaum, S., eds. 1993. *Salem-Village Witchcraft: A Documentary Record of Local Conflict in Colonial New England*, 2nd edn. Boston, Northeastern University Press

Hansen, C. 1969. *Witchcraft at Salem*. New York, George Braziller

Hoffer, P.C. 1997. *The Salem Witchcraft Cases: A Legal History*. Lawrence, University Press of Kansas

Hoffer, P.C. 1998. *The Devil's Disciples: Makers of the Salem Witchcraft Trials*. Baltimore, Johns Hopkins University Press

Lyman Kittredge, G. 1929. *Witchcraft in Old and New England*. Cambridge, MA, Harvard University Press

Norton, M.B. 2002. *In the Devil's Snare*. New York, Alfred A. Knopf

Rosenthal, B. 1993. *Salem Story: Reading the Witch Trials of 1692*. Cambridge, Cambridge University Press

Starkey, M..L. 1969. *The Devil in Massachusetts*. New York, Knopf Doubleday Publishing Group

Acknowledgements

The writing of this book, that is the time spent in front of a computer screen, has taken a relatively short time compared to other books. Nonetheless the putting together of the stories and insights in this book has unequivocally been the work of many years. As such I must express my thanks to the numerous undergraduate and postgraduate students who over three-and-a-half decades have been prepared to discuss these issues with me. Likewise I am grateful to what is now three generations of colleagues who regularly, and unerringly, have never failed to open my eyes to fresh interpretations of new historical insights.

I remain in the debt of a number of specific individuals who have left their mark on some of the contents of this work. I am grateful to my daughter, Bella for her eager and diligent help in compiling the index. I also have academic debts and would like to thank the following individuals in my department for their insight and knowledge: Katherine Watson, Donal Lowry, Glen O'Hara, Tom Crook, Tom Robb, Melanie Reynolds, Adrian Ager, Joanne Bailey, Roger Griffin, Alysa Levene, and Clifford Williamson. I owe a special debt for the help, support, and encouragement always offered to me without question by my friend, colleague, and collaborator on many projects – Anne-Marie Kilday.

Lastly I would like to thank all at Oneworld Publications for their help with getting the manuscript from raw idea to (hopefully polished) publication. In particular I would like to thank Sam Carter for his belief in the value of this manuscript and for his fortitude in seeing it into print.

Index